PRAISE FOR

HOUSEPLANT HORTOCCULTURE

"I am so excited to see Devin share his vast knowledge of the energy and magic of houseplants. His experience working with plants that tend to hail from different areas of the world is respectful, inclusive, and inspiring. This is an essential read for green witches looking to fine-tune their interactions with plants usually seen as indoor and ornamental, from caring for them magically to exploring the lessons the growth cycle and botanical names can teach us. His extensive section on houseplant energies, care, and suggested correspondences is rich, including varieties of a genus and their differences. Don't wait to buy this. You need it right now."

—Arin Murphy-Hiscock, author of *The Green Witch*

"Devin's unique approach to green witchery is the houseplant bible every witch didn't know they needed. The marriage of occultism and houseplants would've been brilliant as is, but Devin went so much deeper, developing a rich and rewarding practice that has completely shifted the way I care for the plants in my own home."

—Lorriane Anderson, best-selling author of *The Witch's Apothecary* and *Seasons of the Witch* oracle decks

"Hunter teaches us to reassess what it means to be magickal and how to see the verdant world in all its potency. This is an important book and will be an eye-opener for many, however *Houseplant Hortocculture* is packed with specific information and so even longtime lovers and cultivators of houseplants like me will find plenty of new information to savor and use. This is a book you will return to again and again."

—Judika Illes, author of *Encyclopedia of 5,000 Spells*

"As many, myself included, focus on the traditional plants of the herbalist, perfumer, and temple gardener, Devin has devoted this book to the familiar yet magickally unfamiliar plants grown in homes across the world....This is a lovely work expanding our perception of green magick to all the plants around us, and it includes practical and esoteric understanding of these plant allies."

—Christopher Penczak, author of *The Plant Spirit Familiar*

"The antidote to a Witch's brown thumb. Smart, witty, with just enough 'you can totally do this' push, Devin Hunter is the magickal best friend nudging the reader to make their magick just a little bit better, wilder, and greener. If you love houseplants and magick, you need this book."

—Courtney Weber, author of *Hekate*

"A must-buy for plant lovers—those in the closet and those out!... People have tried to introduce me to houseplants for years to no avail, but Devin's approach brought it all together—the magic, the practicality, and the healing vibration of houseplants. My 106-year-old Great Mama in spirit is smiling on Devin today and you will too!"

—Michelle Welch, author of *Spirits Unveiled*

"I assumed I didn't have the green touch and should stick to the plastic variety of plants. *Houseplant Hortocculture* has changed my thinking....This practical guide to growing, tending, and maintaining houseplants for magical purposes is inspiring me to get on my broom and head straight to the greenhouse."

—Theresa Reed, author of *The Cards You're Dealt*

"An indispensable guide to the often daunting task of growing plants indoors! Devin Hunter makes the cultivation of houseplants accessible and relatable....Whether you are a grower of indoor poisonous plants, medicinal herbs, or plants with pretty leaves, you will find fertile ground for sowing new seeds within the pages of this book."

—Coby Michael, author of *The Poison Path*

"A thoughtful, thorough, and enjoyable exploration of the green magic we can nurture in our indoor spaces....Adding further value to a book already brimming with it, Hunter provides a beautifully illustrated section of houseplants to help you find new green friends and better care for those already in your home."

—J. R. Mascaro, author of *Seal, Sigil & Call*

"This beautifully illustrated, intimately written guide to the magic of plants is not just a how-to; it is an invitation to relationship."

—Ben Stimpson, author of *Ancestral Whispers*

HOUSEPLANT HORTOCCULTURE

Devin Hunter (San Francisco, CA) is the bestselling author of the *The Witch's Book of Power*, *The Witch's Book of Spirits*, and *The Witch's Book of Mysteries*, as well as the critically acclaimed pictorial formulary *Modern Witch: Spells, Recipes, and Workings* and *Crystal Magic for the Modern Witch*. Initiated into multiple occult orders, Devin is the founder of the Sacred Fires Tradition of Witchcraft and co-founder of the Black Rose Tradition of Witchcraft. He hosts the *Modern Witch* podcast—recommended by both the *AV Club* and *Glamour*—and has been seen on ABC's *To Tell the Truth*. Visit him at ModernWitch.com/Devin.

DEVIN HUNTER

Foreword by Juliet Diaz

HOUSEPLANT HORTOCCULTURE

LLEWELLYN PUBLICATIONS
WOODBURY, MINNESOTA

GREEN MAGIC FOR INDOOR SPACES

FIRST EDITION
First Printing, 2024

Book design by Rebecca Zins
Cover design by Kevin R. Brown
Watercolor illustrations by Siolo Thompson

Library of Congress Cataloging-In-Publication Data
Pending
ISBN 978-0-7387-7397-1

Llewellyn Publications
A Division of Llewellyn Worldwide Ltd.
2143 Wooddale Drive
Woodbury, MN 55125-2989
www.llewellyn.com

PRINTED IN CHINA

MIX
Paper | Supporting responsible forestry
FSC™ C007683

To the green gods, spirits, and allies: may it please you.

To the hundreds of plants I have killed: sorry about that.

To my partner Chas, who I have built a magical indoor and outdoor jungle with: the fella who takes care of my plants when I'm sick or traveling, who tells me when I'm underwatering, and who is always there to encourage my addiction.

To my partner Storm, who is the green devil in my ear constantly demanding more foliage be brought into the house.

To my partner Mat, who married me while I wrote this.
Ha! You're my husband now!

Natural objects themselves, even when they make no claim to beauty, excite the feelings and occupy the imagination. Nature pleases, attracts, delights merely because it is nature. We recognize in it an infinite power.

KARL WILHELM HUMBOLDT

Just because you've only got houseplants doesn't mean you don't have the gardening spirit—I look upon myself as an indoor gardener.

SARA MOSS-WOLFE

My green thumb came only as a result of the mistakes I made while learning to see things from the plant's point of view.

H. FRED DALE

Contents

Foreword

No plant has ever made me feel unworthy of creating a relationship with them. Instead, they have done everything possible to get me to understand that I, myself, am a plant.

I was around seven when I had my first conversation with Aloe Vera. I had just come back home, dirty with mud and dried blood, even pieces of leaves and twigs in my hair; I had spent the day hiding in my favorite oak tree after a group of older kids from my neighborhood chased me with their bikes while throwing rocks at me and yelling *Bruja! Bruja!* Knowing it would slow their bikes, I cut off into a muddy path. One ran when their bikes could no longer move from the mud and caught up to me. He knocked me down, held my face with both hands, looked me straight in the eyes, and said, "You don't belong here."

You don't belong here; I will never forget the hate in his voice and how those words crawled within me, tightening my heart. My mother was not surprised at my chaotic presence because it happened often. She asked me to go and get a piece of the aloe vera sitting by the kitchen window to tend my cuts. As I walked toward them, I stumbled on my slippery, muddy feet and fell right below the windowsill where the plant sat. I had my head down, physically tired and exhausted from people telling me that I did not belong and had no right to exist as I was. *Psst! What's in your pocket?* I was taken aback because no one was in the kitchen with me. I quickly got up and looked around when again the voice said, *What's in your pocket?* This time I knew it was coming from Aloe Vera; I walked closer to them, stuck my little hand in my overall's chest pocket, and pulled out the stones I had collected from the pond I was chased from.

Aloe Vera asked, *Why did you not throw those stones to protect yourself?*

I tilted my head to the side, took a deep breath, thought about it, and said, "Because I would hurt the stones."

Aloe Vera then told me, *Those very stones told me what happened to you, and they also told me how you could have used them to protect yourself but didn't.*

"But how did you talk to the stones?"

Little one, the same way I am talking to you. You can also talk to the stones, as you can also talk to all of nature.

"But how? How can I do that?"

You must understand that you are a plant, stone, tree, animal, mountain, and water; you are everything, for we live in the Spirit that breathes through you because it breathes through us. We are all connected.

"So I belong?"

It's your birthright to belong, little one.

I am sharing this story with you because it is one of many that have saved my life. I have had many hardships, some so bad that I questioned my purpose for even existing. Plants have been my fierce protectors and teachers. They raised me and taught me most of what I know about building a magical relationship with them and working with them for healing, wisdom, spiritual growth, and magical purposes.

Over the years, plants have become popular for their aesthetic, as a competition of who has the most expensive or rare plants just for show. It has taken away the ancestral sacredness of these living beings. Merge that with the capitalistic vultures that could not care less about ethical issues or the spiritual presence of these beings, who are being disrespected and, quite frankly, objectified.

Although I love the aesthetics of plants and geek out when I get ahold of hard-to-find plants, I also don't forget that they are living, breathing beings. Plants that you invite into your home become reflections of the love, care, and healing you give to yourself. They are great allies in your spiritual growth and expansion and fierce weavers in your magical practice. Their ancestral wisdom can transform any season of your life; because of this, they should be honorary guests in your home, not prisoners. The same applies when working with them for magical purposes; they do not owe you anything. Believe me when I say that if your magical workings are not working as powerfully as you would like, disconnection from the plant spirits may be why.

When I met Devin, I was immediately intrigued by his energy—he sure has a lot of plant spirits surrounding him—so naturally, I wanted to become his bestie. Devin and I often text each other to share plant pictures, and we are currently getting ready to exchange plant cuttings from some of our most loved plant babies (I don't give cuttings to just anyone; I am incredibly protective of them). I have found through our conversations that Devin truly is a plant papi; he loves, cherishes, and respects his plants. Not only is Devin incredibly knowledgeable about plants, but he is also eager to learn more, which is one of the reasons I trust his work. He has been a great friend to me and respects my culture and the wisdom it carries. When I sent him a recording for his online hortocculture event, he told me that after seeing the video he knew I was a real one, and I want to say that Devin, you are a real one too.

The amount of work that he put into this book is impressive, from caring for the plant to which tarot card they connect to (excuse me, what!?). *Above and beyond* were my first thoughts when reading through this book. I love that he created a work that is unique and personal to him. Because of this, he was able to bring you knowledge from experience and the intimate relationships he has with the plants he shares. This kind of wisdom is powerful in helping you, the reader, connect to the plants more in-depth. He also did an incredible job merging the occult connection with the plants to help amplify your magic and magical workings. Nothing about this book is repeated content that we often see in many herbal or plant books. And my favorite part as an indigenous woman is that he does not appropriate other cultures and respectfully speaks on this in this book. We need more writers like Devin to be an example of how we can coexist and not cross boundaries while being in community and helping each other elevate our individual practices. If you know of my work, you know that this is how I approach my teachings—by teaching the reader to build something unique and powerful for themselves that aligns with them. This is how we access our most powerful magic.

Devin has created a book that is intentional and mindful and one that I know his plant friends are doing a happy dance over. This book is full of suggested workings and various practices to connect even those who don't think they have a green thumb to the world of hortocculture. This book empowers beginners and is an excellent guide for more advanced practitioners. As an experienced plant brujera, I know many of the techniques in this book are not techniques I or anyone would find anywhere else. Because of this, and with everything I shared that I love about this book, it should be on every plant lover's shelf.

Juliet Diaz
INDIGENOUS SEER AND PLANT BRUJERA

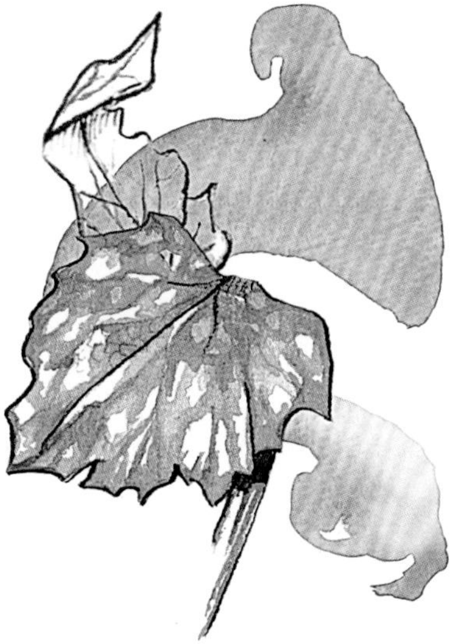

Introduction

I have always been a bit of an outsider when it comes to the plants I have been attracted to work with in magic. While other witches were off potting mandrake, salvia, and other classically associated plants that come to mind when you think of the occult, I was playing with colocasia and philodendron. It wasn't that I didn't have an appreciation for the outdoors (if anything, my love of the outdoors prompted my interest in houseplants), but I wanted to bring nature inside my home and saw great potential in doing so as a magician. When I would mention my interest in houseplants to other witches, I would often be met with a bit of disregard—"they are just houseplants"—and one teacher even said, "I only grow plants I can use in magic."

These conversations haunt me, reemerging every time I walk into a garden center or add a new plant to my collection. No plant is ever "just a houseplant," and I have dedicated a big part of my own spiritual and magical life to proving it, if only to myself. Unlike the herbs, trees, and baneful plants that we most often associate with magic, houseplants don't generally carry the same weight in our occult studies, and I believe that is because we have "othered" them as outsiders and unknowns.

The plants traditionally assumed to be magical typically have a body of lore and a history of prior use that is well documented in the West. Think of lavender and willow, for example, both of which make appearances in ancient Greek tales and medicine and whose attributes have changed little since those times. On the other hand, the same cannot be said for many houseplants, whose origins are typically far from the West and are of recent discovery or cultivation. Which brings me to my second point.

A lot—and I mean *a lot*—of these plants originate in tropical and subtropical places like South America, China, and on small island nations where magical traditions like we have in the West do not exist. This isn't at all saying they don't have their own magical traditions, merely that magic in these places exists in a very different way to the indigenous peoples of these areas than it does for us in the West. For us, we have to seek out magic; for them, it is simply everywhere. Many of these peoples still remain undivorced from plant life in ways that we simply are not accustomed to.

While we would be fools to ignore any wisdom these people might have to freely share with us as to the magical properties of these plants, the overwhelming sentiment from those I talk to seems to be that we can figure it out for ourselves. It isn't that these cultures have no wisdom to share; rather, it isn't ours to take from, and it simply wouldn't make sense outside of their own contexts.

Before we go any further, let me make one thing abundantly clear as to my purpose and intention with this book: I will not be sharing any information regarding indigenous practices that are related to the plants I discuss here. Not only is it not my place to share such information, but also it would be incredibly presumptuous to think I could speak from a place of authority on the subject. Those mysteries, if they exist, are for those peoples to explore with the rest of the world when and if they are ready. What I present to you here is my completely unrelated gnosis with the utmost respect to these peoples.

I think the general lack of familiarity and classical reference makes houseplants foreigners to a lot of people in the magical community. We are so focused on tradition in occultism that we sometimes forget to create new traditions or take what we have learned elsewhere and apply it in the face of new discoveries. In few places is this so glaringly apparent as when it comes to the magical potential of houseplants.

I speak of building new traditions, but the truth is, houseplants are nothing new. There is evidence that humans have had houseplants since at least 600 BCE,[1] if not earlier. In this time there have been plenty of traditions created that we can look at for guidance. And, as I mentioned before, we can apply the already ample wisdom related to other plants to those we might grow inside the home.

While we will get into semantics later, what makes a houseplant a houseplant is that you can provide the conditions necessary for its survival inside your home. That means literally any plant can be a houseplant. The plants we will be discussing in this book are those which are in cultivation and whose evolution in some cases has been guided by human hands. While I will focus on plants that are commonly known as houseplants and who have been cultivated for their use indoors, I am also going to introduce you to plants that aren't typically thought of as houseplants because they require a little more attention than your average plant found at the supermarket or garden center.

While I won't be able to cover every houseplant or magical practice related to them, I will be doing my best to cover species that are common throughout the world and give you the tools necessary to crack the code on any related plants that you might find out in the world. Once you understand what a plant species is capable of, inferring what the individual subspecies and their relatives are capable of is actually pretty easy.

1 Camilleri and Kaplan, *Plantopedia*, 12.

In addition to tackling the idea of houseplants as being foreign to green magic and introducing you to what I have learned about their magical properties, I am also going to share with you as much information as I can about how to keep your plants healthy and alive so that the magic you do with them can truly thrive!

As it stands now, my partner Chas and I are the caretakers of over twelve hundred very magical houseplants. Living in the suburbs, it became a goal of ours to re-wild our space and bring as much nature inside as possible. Over the years what started off as a pothos in the corner has turned into a home brimming to the edges with plants.

In 2020 this all came to a head when we joined the rest of the world in self-quarantine as shelter-in-place orders took effect in our area. Days turned to months, and I found myself dealing with a deep depression. In addition to what was going on around me, my internal world felt chaotic and turbulent. People I loved were passing away. My business had to close the doors to its physical location after thirty years. I couldn't go anywhere or see anyone. We had a plant or two in every room, but we hadn't been bitten by the bug just yet.

One morning, not too far into the pandemic, I woke to find that my *Colocasia* 'Black Ruffles' had died. It had been a pet project of mine and had been the only thing on some days that I was willing to get out of bed to take care of. As I looked at the wilted mass of goop that it had turned into, my heart finally gave way and the tears I had not allowed myself to shed came pouring out. There I was, a grown man in his thirties, crying over a dead plant. Of course, it wasn't about the plant but instead what the plant symbolized for me in the moment. It was life as I knew it—and I had killed it.

I felt horrible for killing it, but I also felt horrible for being such a mess that I hadn't seen the warning signs that there was a problem.

"You can get another," my partner said as he stepped in to see what the sobbing was about. "It sucks, but I just killed two of my plants, too. It isn't like it is a dog or a person. You can get another and try again."

He was right. Just like life, I could begin anew. And so, after much moaning, I did. When I got the replacement, I fell in love all over again and this time paid a little more attention to it. Once it was healthy and happy, I started adding more plants to my personal collection until they spilled out into the halls and eventually the rest of the house. With each plant I got a new opportunity to explore life—my life—and as I took care of them, they started to take care of me. I traded cuttings of my plants for others to expand my collection and learned to care for species that required special care, like me. Before I knew it, I found myself feeling whole again; each new leaf was a new beginning, and each fading leaf was a cycle coming to a close. In a time when death permeated everything, I somehow filled myself and my magic with life.

No matter the traditions we do speak of or the spells that are shared, my wish is that you find the keys necessary for you to do the same in your life. While it is my firm belief that every plant is magical, I also believe that those plants you grow and surround yourself with are especially magical. It is my great honor to dive into this topic with you and that you have chosen me to be your guide.

In part 1 we explore the layers and nuances of working with the plant kingdom as spiritual and magical partners. We will discuss their spirits, their care needs and how to approach those needs with magic in mind, and the many ways that you can anchor their magic in your life. In the second part we will explore almost two hundred species and their magical correspondences as well as what makes them especially suited for life in your home.

Before we jump in, I would like to suggest that you keep a journal handy as you read along. Take notes, but also write down your own impressions and record the conclusions you draw. My ultimate goal is that you feel confident in adding any plant you are growing (or want to grow) into your magical practice. Much of this will come from the insight you receive while reading.

This book was written for the magical practitioner who possesses a basic to intermediate level of understanding about witchcraft. If, by chance, this is your first book on the craft, I recommend checking out ModernWitch.com, my website, for more information on magic and the occult. You'll find plenty of free resources, lessons, and other material that will answer any questions you might have about the basics. I also invite you to check out the bibliography and recommended reading section in the back of this book, where you will find a plethora of reference material.

Without further ado, I present to you houseplant hortocculture.

PART ONE

HORTOCCULTURAL *HAPPENINGS*

I do not yet know why plants come out of the land or float in streams, or creep on rocks or roll from the sea. I am entranced by the mystery of them and absorbed by their variety and kinds. Everywhere they are visible yet everywhere occult.

LIBERTY HYDE BAILEY

I had originally intended to start this section off with some plant care horror stories. But as I typed them up, I realized that introducing you to the topic of plant care with nightmare fuel probably wouldn't be effective in the way I would like. It also dawned on me that you probably have plenty of your own horror stories about accidentally murdering a houseplant, and who am I to dredge up those memories you have worked so hard at burying? So instead, my friend, I am going to come out and say something that few would say to your face: plants die, and sometimes it is your fault.

It sucks. It can be costly. It can be a maddening catastrophe that drives you far from ever wanting to take care of a plant again. But it happens. No matter how long you have been raising plants and caring for them, regardless of how wise and green your thumb, you are going to kill a plant or two every now and then. The joke among gardeners is that the longer you do this activity, it isn't that your odds of killing a plant decrease, but rather the likelihood of killing an expensive plant will increase. We all want to show off our successes to the world, but I guarantee you that behind those successes have been a lot of failures. So, if you are one of those people who have accidentally killed a plant or gave your plant away because it was on the brink of death, I want you to know that you aren't alone. We all do that. And as we will discuss later, it might not have been your fault.

The death of a plant you are working with for magical purposes is doubly hard because you cannot help but look at the loss as an extension of your success as spellcaster. Indeed, as we will be exploring throughout this entire book, plants worked with in this way do become the embodiment of your magic, just as much if not more than any statue or magical tool. Furthermore, unlike working with herbs or garden plants, the point is to keep a houseplant alive, not cut up, and then dry out its corpse for later use. We need our magical houseplants alive and thriving!

The green flame is the psychic/spiritual force behind all plant life, and we will be learning to be its priests/esses/exes. It is the unrelenting push of nature to carry out life wherever it can as the sustaining giver that allows complex life to evolve. Those who raise plants indoors have effectively scooped up a tiny bit of that green flame and brought it into their homes. They tend to it, love it, talk to it, and learn its secrets. In time their collection grows, and their homes become verdant temples of the green flame. I can't think of many things that are witchier or more occult than that.

In part 1 we are going to discuss all of the things necessary for you to successfully raise magical houseplants with confidence and embrace the green flame as a sacred wielder of its magic. While it might get a little sciency here and there, knowing how to care for the plants we work with in our magic is just as important as the work we do with them in magic. Unlike stones or tarot cards, these are living, breathing things that require good stewardship if they are to make strong allies.

We will, of course, be approaching the subject of plant care as occultists and taking advantage of opportunities for us to apply magical techniques and practices to not only improve our chance of success, but lay the bedrock for deeper possible magics like those discussed in the later parts of the book. Our goal isn't just to stop killing plants or merely keep them alive, but rather to learn what it takes to help them thrive in every way. This is important not just as people who don't want to murder plants, but as magicians who need our allies to stay alive as well as have all the tools needed to be successful at the magic we've partnered with them to perform.

Chapter One

The Green Flame

O most honored Greening Force,
You who roots in the Sun;
You who lights up, in shining serenity, within a wheel
that earthly excellence fails to comprehend.
You are enfolded
in the weaving of divine mysteries.
You redden like the dawn
and You burn: flame of the Sun.

. . .

Hildegard von Bingen, *Causae et Curae*

Houseplant hortocculture is a fun play on words I came up with to describe the community of occultists and spiritual types who have incorporated green magic and green wisdom into their lives via houseplants, as well as the unique practices that work entails. I like to think of it as a lifestyle as much as a part of my spiritual path, and I am not alone! Hortocculture is about more than just the spells and rituals we can perform with plants.

At its root it is about developing a spiritual relationship with plants that allows us access to the otherwise hidden and unseen elements of life and, of course, magic.

The reason I call houseplant hortocculture a lifestyle is because it requires us to incorporate what we learn and practice into our daily lives in real time. I mean, houseplants don't exactly take care of themselves. We fill our homes with them, we fill our time with their care, and we find little pieces of ourselves along the way. When we add the layer of spiritual connection, that relationship grows to become much deeper than one expects possible. Trust me. I know from personal experience.

Having a spiritual connection to plants is nothing new in occultism, but usually the topic is solely focused on herbs, crops, trees, and medicinal plants—plants that, in all actuality, aren't necessarily something that someone who lives in a concrete jungle, the suburbs, or a tiny apartment can easily grow. Nor are they necessarily plants that call to everyone. I grew up in rural Ohio, where every summer we grew and then canned the vegetables that we would rely upon the following fall and winter. While that might sound like a lot of fun to some, you very well may be one of the millions of people for whom that sounds like a nightmare. I promise you it certainly isn't everyone's cup of tea. All these plants, however, generally remain firmly as outdoor facets, aside from the occasional kitchen window herb box.

Houseplants, on the other hand, are plants that we invite into our homes. They are our way of meeting Mother Nature halfway. In witchcraft and occultism, talk regarding plants is always about going out into nature, but sometimes we have to bring nature to us. Houseplant hortocculture allows us as spiritual types to make space for Mother Nature even when we can't build a home in the middle of the woods and become the mad old wizards and witches of our dreams. Sometimes life is all about making the best out of option B.

By no means am I suggesting that raising houseplants is a replacement for going out and making friends with your local plants and ecosystems. But I am saying that you can open your doors to the spirit of the wild—and that, in my experience, familiarizing yourself with a houseplant is usually the gateway for developing a connection to the natural environment outside your home. Even if houseplants don't lead you to becoming a master gardener, they will still guide you to having a deeper, more meaningful relationship with our planet. And that, my friends, is worth more than the rarest philodendron.

The Green Flame

Working with plants as an occultist will instantly put you in contact with the omnipresent force of nature that I refer to as the green flame.[2] All plant life is of the green flame, and you have undoubtedly noticed it. We can see it in the activity of the spring when plants come out of dormancy, at the peak of summer when their foliage is full and luscious, in the blade of grass that sprouts up through the pavement, and in the forests that reclaim abandoned places. It is the power of nature to overcome any obstacle and its fighting spirit to survive.

As a force of nature, it is neither good nor bad nor bound to unmoving thought. It simply exists as a force like any other in the universe, and as psychic beings capable of perceiving and channeling spiritual energies, we are capable of working with it in our magic and spirituality. Why would we want to do this? Well, as I mentioned earlier, it is our way of letting nature into our lives and meeting it halfway. Beyond that, however, the green flame is wild and free; it is not something we ever tame but rather something we make friends

2 In my books *The Witch's Book of Mysteries* and *Crystal Magic for the Modern Witch*, I discuss the other flames at length. The green flame is one of nine traditional flames that are seen as divisions of a whole, similar to how light divides into a spectrum. Each flame is a spiritual piece of the universe, an essential element of its makeup.

with. Working with it is part of our spiritual inheritance as the descendants of an agricultural society and a hunter-gatherer society before that. As people who eat, the green flame is part of our lives and the lives of our ancestors, even if we are removed from it by a few degrees of separation. Our ancestors knew this wild force—they knew the spirits who served it and embodied its traits—and now it is our turn.

We will revisit the concept of the green flame over and over again, but let's get the ball rolling by psychically connecting to it and then channeling it. Once we have that down, the rest is easy! For now, let's focus on feeling and sensing our way through the green flame as a force of nature.

Connecting to the Green Flame

If you have ever pretended to be Poison Ivy from DC's *Batman*, this is all going to be a breeze! Grab a plant and hold it in your hands. Visualize it growing from a shoot to a stalk and then the leaves filling out. In your mind's eye, see the plant grow from seedling to full maturity. As you do this, tune in with all your senses and check in with your mind, body, and spirit. Look for sensations that you can relate to what you see in your mind.

Those sensations are all potential avenues that can help you access this energy later, so make notes of those that do come to you while you do this practice. Try this again with at least two other plants and then compare your notes. Which sensations were present in the majority of your experiences? Those sensations are likely representative for you of the green flame and can be called upon later through memory to help you access it with ease.

If you are able, go to a park or a wild place and connect similarly to the trees and plants there. Touch them, tune in, and use your psychic senses to create a brief profile, then compare those notes to what you have already recorded. What were the similarities between the plants you have at home and those in the wild? Those are further indicators of what exactly we are talking about when we discuss this force. Because we all experience the psychic and spiritual through our own unique lens, trust your intuition and feel your way through this process.

Distill these sensations into two or three keywords that can help you describe your personal understanding of the green flame. For me, these words are *pervasive*, *verdant*, and *life*. These keywords are what I chant when I want to tune in quickly to the green flame. I repeat them until I feel the presence of this force enter my psychic space. For me, this feels like being plugged into a fast and excited biological machine. For my friend, it is a sudden feeling of relaxation that is accompanied by a feeling of harmony. Same force, different people. Perform this connection a few times and observe how this happens for you.

Channeling the Green Flame

We can take it to the next level and channel the green flame. By this, I mean we can focus that energy with our mind and spirit and give it direction. To do this, connect as before, chanting those three words and using their related sensations to help you remember the feeling of what it is like to be in the presence of the green flame in action. Once you have done this, visualize that energy manifesting in your personal space as a ball of emerald-green electric fire that hovers just outside the center of your chest. Now spend a few moments simply feeling this all out and allowing the ball of energy to grow comfortably.

Next, we want to draw that energy outward by taking the index and middle fingers of your dominant hand and tapping the sphere that is hovering in front of your heart. Gently pull away and bring your hand down to your side. As you do this, visualize a trail of green fire following your fingers as if you had dipped them in paint and the air were a canvas.

At this point, you can charge candles or plants with this energy or work with it in some other magic, but for now let's disconnect. We will revisit this work in the following chapters.

To disconnect from the green flame and end the channeling session, bring your index and middle finger back to the sphere in front of your heart and tap once more. When you do this, visualize the connection between the two severing. Take three deep breaths and visualize the ball of green flame being absorbed into your body and then traveling through your energy centers until it exits through your feet and finally is absorbed into the ground beneath you.

Your Green Thumb

We have all heard the term "green thumb" used to describe the ability to take care of plants successfully. It is something we say others have when they can keep more than one plant alive and something we say we *don't* have when we kill our first. Aside from whether or not you have a history of being a plant murderer, a green thumb is something that you can grow like any other aspect of the green flame, and witchcraft can help with that. Well, more to the point, your witchcraft practice can provide you with opportunities to grow one.

In truth, a green thumb is nothing more than a skill that is picked up over time through a lot of experience and having an intuitive understanding of plant life. This intuitive understanding isn't a second sense, however. It is the ability to comprehend what a plant needs and then instinctively respond to those needs. Over time this becomes second nature, something that develops as you grow alongside the plants you care for. If you are capable of being present while caring for them and can draw wisdom from your experiences, then growing a green thumb isn't such a difficult task.

As witches and occultists, however, we must take a look at the spiritual and psychic elements of having a green thumb. The green thumb is something that develops almost as a side effect of becoming deeply connected to the plant kingdom and the green flame. So, the more we fuse elements of our plant care and our interactions with plants with our spiritual or magical practice, the stronger our green thumbs become.

Throughout this book we are going to explore these topics in as much detail as possible. We will discuss everything from working with the deities and spirits associated with our houseplants to how to care for them as an act of devotion, and even how to develop a long term and meaningful spiritual practice with them. But before we go into all that, I want to take a moment to address those folks out there who are resistant or feeling trepidatious because maybe in the past you have killed a plant or two or haven't had much luck spiritually and psychically connecting to plants.

The Twelve Easiest Houseplants to Get Witchy With

I have this theory that most of the people who think they can't successfully raise plants for the fun of it, let alone include in a spiritual practice, have most likely not been working with the right plants. I mean that both in the woo-woo sense that those plants might not have been copasetic with that person's energy and also in a very practical sense. Not all houseplants are good for beginners, and not all beginners are good for every houseplant! There are dozens of factors that can make for a bad first (or third or fourth) experience.

Many of us find a plant that we like because it looks pretty and assume that because we took fifth grade biology and saw a botanical documentary at two in the morning, we can take care of it—when in reality the pretty plant is likely something that requires an environment we simply cannot provide. Many plants sold in grocery stores, hardware stores, and even nurseries are not ideal plants for beginners, and many of them will end up dying in those stores from lack of care. For all you know, you got a plant that was already on its way out. All of this to say, there is a good chance that the odds were stacked against you. But we can fix that if you are willing to give it another chance.

To those who haven't had luck spiritually or psychically connecting to a plant in the past, I say the same thing: chances are the odds were stacked against you. Not all plant energies and spirits make themselves known easily. In my experience, most of them don't trust humanity a whole lot and can take some warming up before they make themselves known.

There are plants that are easier to grow, connect with, and care for that are excellent allies to get your bearings with. Here are twelve that I recommend to both beginner houseplant enthusiasts and those beginning their spiritual journey with plants. These are easy on all fronts, and their related spirits are not shy. Some of these I will go into more detail with in part 2; however, you can find more about how to care for them in chapter 4.

POTHOS (EPIPREMNUM): A small fast-growing trailing plant that is an excellent partner in magic for opportunity, love, and success. Let its pot dry out 50 percent before watering thoroughly. Its number one issue is overwatering.

ALOE: A succulent favorite in many homes that is great for healing magic and soothing tempers. Put it in a window and only water it once the soil has dried out. Overwatering is its most common care concern.

KALANCHOE: Also known as paddle plant, this is another succulent that prefers to dry out completely before being thoroughly watered. It is a fantastic partner in magic related to finances.

SYNGONIUM: A fast-growing, all-purpose magic plant that brings focus and acuity to spells and rituals. Water when the top inch of the soil is dry.

PILEA PEPEROMIOIDES (CHINESE MONEY PLANT): Excellent for drawing new streams of income and opportunities for financial growth. Water thoroughly when the leaves begin to droop.

SPIDER PLANT: An easy-to-grow hanging plant that enjoys bright indirect light and having the soil dry out 50 percent between waterings. Grow this plant to bring new ideas and inspire creativity.

PEACE LILY: Can handle low-light environments and has air-purifying properties. Water when the top inch of soil is dry or when the leaves begin to droop. Work with this plant to bring peace and serenity into the home.

DRACAENA: Can grow in multiple locations around the home with ease. Allow the soil to dry out 50 percent in between waterings. Grow for protection and to keep yourself from being seen by those you wish to remain hidden from.

SANSEVIERIA (THE SNAKE PLANT): Excellent for cutting through issues and removing obstacles. Allow to dry out 50 percent between thorough waterings.

ZAMIOCULCAS (THE ZZ PLANT): This is a great partner in magic related to spirit guides. Allow to dry out 50 percent between thorough waterings.

MONSTERA: The *Monstera deliciosa* specifically is excellent in magic related to being seen and drawing attention. Grow in chunky, well-draining soil and allow to dry out 25 percent between waterings.

AGLAONEMA (CHINESE EVERGREEN): The perfect partner in magic related to luck and good fortune. Water when the soil has dried out 50 percent.

Green Gnosis

PART ONE

If you have never read one of my books before, then you do not know of my insatiable love for a journal. Throughout each chapter we are going to discuss a lot of topics that can feel like background information but are actually vital concepts for us to understand if we are to have any deep connection with our subject. At the end of each chapter, you will see a section called Green Gnosis where you are invited to interact with the material by journaling about your interpretations and experiences regarding what we just discussed. If you follow along and participate in each prompt, then at the end of part 1 you will have a fully fleshed-out green magic practice that centers solely on your houseplants.

Please respond to the following questions in your journal. Be as sincere and honest in your responses as possible, and feel free to revisit them as you move throughout the book and touch on more topics.

» *What attracts you to caring for houseplants? What about it makes you excited?*

» *What is your earliest memory of seeing or feeling the energy of the green flame in your life?*

» *What were the three words you chose to define your interpretation of the green flame?*

» *In your opinion, what does a healthy plant feel like energetically compared to one that is not doing well or is dead?*

» *What houseplants have you had the most success with, and why do you think that is? If you haven't had much experience, what is a houseplant that you have seen others grow successfully, and why do you think that is?*

Chapter Two

Green Spirits

> There may be fairies at the bottom of the garden. There is no evidence for it, but you can't prove that there aren't any, so shouldn't we be agnostic with respect to fairies?
>
> Richard Dawkins

For me, occultism begins and ends with the world of spirits. I am a medium, which means I came preprogrammed with the ability to communicate with them. It wasn't something that I asked for—it was just there, getting me into trouble from a young age. When I began my journey with houseplants and started to fill my home with them, I quickly learned that there was an entire family of green spirits that I would be working with. As a houseplant hortocculturist, there are many different spirits that you might run into and even a few you might want to invite. In this chapter we are going to explore the relationship that plants have with the spiritual world, the consciousness within them, and how we as witches and occultists might work with those forces in partnership.

Green Guides

Green guides are spirit guides who are devoted to helping us establish a connection with the planet through the cultivation of plants and restoration of the environment. They are spirits that can help us understand what our plants need, and they can act as ambassadors for us in the plant world. Whenever I have a problem with my plants, I check in with my green guides and ask them to assist in developing the best care practices possible.

In more than one instance, they have alerted me to problems that were happening with my collection and are responsible for saving a lot of plants over the years. They also help us make connections with other green spirits, such as the one we will talk about next, who might be difficult to contact.

Admittedly, my green guides didn't just pop up out of the ground one day. I had to go looking for them. I had been working with a rare alocasia that was failing after importing, and I asked another alocasia what it thought I should do. "Get a guide," it said, and showed me the following working.

To Summon a Green Guide

While facing the direction of the rising sun, light a green candle. Trace a circle of green fire in the air before you by using the index and middle finger of your dominant hand and visualize a green flame pouring from your fingertips. Take a deep breath. As you exhale, visualize the ring of green flame burning as though it were being pulled into the center of the circle, and then say aloud the following incantation:

> Hear me, spirits of the green flame,
> For I am a child of the earth.
> I seek a guide who is wise and verdant
> One who knows their worth.
> I summon a companion, friend, and mentor

Who speaks a language of green,
An eager ally from the hedge
Who dances betwixt and between.

Allow the candle to burn down on its own, and when it does finally go out, return to the circle of green flame. Take three deep breaths, and with each exhale visualize the ring dissolving and then being absorbed by your plants. Take a few moments to check in with yourself and your surroundings. If you don't sense a presence right away, no worries! It took me a few days to notice that I had extra helpers around.

Working with Your Green Guides

The general rule of thumb is that guides are here to guide us. They can't hurt us or steer us into harm's way; they exist as mentors and mediators. Because our green guides are hardwired for helping, we can work with them for guidance in just about any related situation. Where exactly do they come from? In this case, we used the green flame to connect to them, which means our guides will be high-vibrational beings connected to the universal force responsible for plant life.

Approaching them doesn't have to be difficult, especially if you have done the previous working. I like to take a few moments to ground and center myself so I can be fully in the moment, and then I call on them to help me before I begin my plant care routine. You might expect my call to them to be something fancy, but in truth I just kind of say, "Are you ready to get to work?" and they always show up. Having your green guides with you when you are going around and taking care of your plants is an excellent way to build up your relationship over time. On the other hand, they can also be incredibly helpful outside of your normal regimen!

Green Guides in Action

Our green guides aren't just here to help us take care of our plants; they are here to help us become better acquainted with the green flame and the plant kingdom. The relationship you develop with them inside your home when you are taking care of your houseplants also extends far beyond your home's confines. Here are three times when you should definitely check in with your green guides.

When Shopping for New Plants

Once you get into houseplants, it can become quite addictive. I found myself wanting every plant I came across, but not all those plants were actually good fits for my home! After money lost, time spent, and feelings of failure while watching an expensive plant die, I learned to ask my green guides for help. Instead of assuming I could learn to take care of it and give it whatever it might need, I started asking if my home and my limited time were going to be enough to take care of the plant. Sometimes it isn't that you can't provide for the plant's needs; rather, you may not have adequate time to take care of it or your life changes and suddenly taking care of a more needful plant becomes too difficult.

Ask your green guides if the plant is a good fit and if you are in the right place in your life to take care of it. I know they say intention is all that matters in witchcraft, but plants are here to show us otherwise! It takes more than our intention to be good magical plant parents to actually *be* good magical plant parents.

When You Feel Overwhelmed

Plants are awesome, and this whole book is a celebration of them, but sometimes taking care of them can be overwhelming. What starts off as a nice relaxing hobby can quickly turn into a stressful chore. This becomes more and more of an issue with each new plant variety you bring into your collection. As you diversify, care needs will diversify, and this can lead to more demands on your time and attention. A plant can be fine one day and then the next you discover it is covered in mites and needs your immediate attention. All of this is normal for plant care, but it can add pressure to your life if you are already feeling stressed, run-down, or depressed. Yes, plants can be therapeutic to work with, but more isn't necessarily better.

When you feel overwhelmed in life or by your plant collection, turn to your green guides for help invigorating your practice so that it serves both you and your plants. Ask for help from them when you need it; that is what they are there for.

When You Need to Make Connections to Other Green Spirits

My last little reminder about green guides is that they are mediators for us and the plant world. If you have a problem connecting to a concept or a particular spirit within the plant kingdom, turn to your green guides for an introduction.

Plant Spirits

We are going to discuss many different topics, techniques, and methods throughout the next few hundred pages, and almost all of them will circle back to the idea and concept of what we refer to as the "plant spirit." The plant spirit is the sentience that we communicate with and develop a relationship to each time we work with a specific plant. For each individual species there is an individual plant spirit that is shared throughout. That means that all *Monstera deliciosa* plants share a common plant spirit. When a plant mutates and becomes a new epithet, or species, the plant spirit does the same. A newer, mutated version of the spirit springs to life along with the new physical mutation. That means a variegated *Monstera deliciosa* has a different version of the plant spirit because of its mutation, but those spirits are related, like sisters. They share very similar properties but have their own personalities and looks. For each different botanical name that you can find, you can bet your buttons there is a plant spirit waiting to be discovered.

To be frank, the best thing you can do to develop that relationship is to take good care of the plant. Chapter 4 is solely dedicated to magical houseplant care with this in mind. We have to look at our plant care as an act of devotion to the plant spirit and the green flame. Aside from that, I leave them offerings of gemstones in their pots and sometimes get them fancy bottled water or spend extra money on a really nice pot for them to be in when I "up pot" them. I do whatever I can to make the most inviting space for that spirit to visit and treat each plant's container as an altar to its plant spirit (more on this later).

Houseplants are mostly subtropical plants that hail from South America and Asia. These are plants that naturally do well in our average home temperatures and are better suited for life in our homes than plants from other temperate regions. When exploring the topic of plant spirits, we usually look for the myths and stories that surround them in their native habitats, but that gets quite tricky once we get into houseplants. As I mentioned in the introduction, we won't be diving into indigenous plant spirit medicine or mysteries in this book, despite plant spirits being such a big part of the practices discussed here. Let's take a moment to talk about why.

The greatest threat we can bring to this topic is assumption. Traditional Western occultism is full of assumption, and we tend to project those assumptions onto any and everything we come across. We assume that because we have a well-developed and explored folkloric system for plant magic that every magical culture must have one as well and that it will fit neatly into our own because our system works so well for us. That is rarely the case, especially when discussing plant spirituality. We also tend to assume that it is okay to take what works from one culture and apply it to our own. Again, this is rarely the case.

When we look to the peoples indigenous to the places where most of our houseplants come from, we find a very different approach to life and magic than our own. These peoples have a rich and beautiful connection to the land and the plants that grow there and see them not as a tool or something to exploit, but more as a part of the natural landscape. Yes, there are mysteries and magics that developed within these cultures for some plants, but most of them are intricately connected to the land itself and are specific to that region and culture. To even attempt to explore those things outside of that context will result in a gross overreach on our part as occultists who are not part of those communities, and we could not possibly understand them without respectfully immersing ourselves in those cultures. For that, you most certainly would need an invitation. In Western occultism, when we try to fit things like this into our system, we almost always change it for the worse as we can't help but alter meaning in the translation. We then end up sharing this altered information with others and colonizing the original system with our altered version of things. The more those altered versions spread, the less the entire system looks like the original. We really step in it when we claim to be authority figures on the topic as outsiders who promote the altered version, so let's just avoid that mess altogether.

The other reason that applying mysteries or magics to these plants based on their place of origin is problematic is that the average houseplant has been in cultivation for so long that it might as well be a different plant in some cases. The history of indoor plants goes back thousands of years, but it has been a fairly popular practice since the Victorian era. During this time breeders have created hybrids that are more suitable for our homes and lifestyles. So even if a plant like the *Philodendron erubescens* hails from South America, breeders in

Thailand have created incredible hybrids and crossbred similar species to bring out the most visually appealing traits possible. Then a breeder in Germany gets one of those and produces an entirely new species of philodendron by crossbreeding the *Philodendron erubescens* with *Philodendron gloriosum* (difficult but not impossible). These things would not happen naturally in the wild; they could only be the result of human influence. Furthermore, some of those plants wouldn't survive in nature without human intervention, such is the case with many, such as the *Monstera deliciosa* 'Albo variegata'.

I decided years ago that instead of inviting myself into indigenous plant mysteries, I was going to invite those plants into my mysteries and began studying them using my own set of tools. What I present to you on the topic of plant spirits and magic related to these species is entirely my own gnosis presented with the utmost respect to the cultures who live and come from the areas where these plants originate. I do not present to you their mysteries or traditions but my own that were developed over time through my practices as a witch, occultist, and medium. Now, let's get on with it!

The Plant Pantheon

The next group of friends I am going to introduce you to are larger than life and can be a little difficult to explain. Let's cover a few of their commonalities to better help us wrap our heads around what it is that we are actually talking about.

For starters, you have already met these divine beings. You know them from common sayings, art, advertising, and history. They are personifications of nature that are often given human features but aren't human in the slightest. We have a habit of assigning things like fixed gender and even skin tone to them, and I think that is a big mistake. The best possible thing we can do as we embark on working with the plant kingdom is to shed what we think we know about these spirits and let them present themselves to us as they would see fit. That is the only way to develop an old-fashioned authentic relationship with them.

These beings transcend culture and pop up in one form or another all over the world throughout time. They mean something different to each group of people who interprets their presence. Feel free to swap out any language in these prayers/invocations to fit your personal vision of these spirits. They won't mind, I promise. While these spirits/deities are usually relegated to the outdoor places, we will be making an effort to bring them indoor as we raise our collection of magical houseplants.

Mother Nature

EARTH MOTHER, BRINGER OF FOLIAGE, SLAYER OF CITIES

I know that Mother Nature is a fun euphemism for a lot of people, but for occultists the term describes a very real presence in the universe. Like most things in the occult, a deep look reveals cosmic implications, but to keep things grounded we are going to focus on Mother Nature as the Earth Mother or Gaia, a being who is very much the spirit of our planet. While not solely a spirit of the green flame, Mother Nature is most certainly part of the green flame.

We call the spirit of our planet Earth Mother or Mother Nature because life as we know it sprang forth from it. It shelters us as a mother would, it teaches us as a mother would, and it provides for us as a mother would. Believe it or not, the soul of our planet cares about you; it cares about each of us. The only question is, do you care about it?

Green magic in general helps us better understand and connect to Mother Nature, but houseplant magic affords us a rare opportunity to bring Mother Nature into our homes. By raising houseplants, we are meeting Mother Nature halfway and making space for her in real time. Don't get me wrong; this isn't a substitute for the real deal, but I wholeheartedly believe it is both an acceptable alternative and a good step in the right direction.

A Prayer to the Earth Mother

Mother Nature, I lift my thoughts to you. I awaken the green flame within and devote its light to your service. I guard this flame. I cherish this flame as an act of devotion and an act of love, for you bless us with water to drink, air to breathe, sustenance to eat, and from you all creation springs forth. Unto you all things return after life, and from their remains you make rich soils and fertile land. You are the verdant fields and the dense jungle, the roaring volcano and the ocean deep. You are the maker of delicate flowers and venomous teeth, the composer of rain and drought, the mother of countless souls and the reaper of unending beauty. Bless and guide me; help me find my way to you. Help me rise to your standard so I may be the best steward of your mysteries. Blessed be.

The Green Man

The term *Green Man* is a more recent invention to describe a very real cultural deity found all throughout Europe during the medieval era and can even be found as far as places like Lebanon. Though it is believed his roots are in the pre-Christian world and that he is likely most related to Bacchus, his popularity skyrocketed during the thirteenth century in what is now the United Kingdom, and he can be seen in church motifs all throughout the country. He is seen as the spirit of the wild, a very real part of everyday life for the common person.

A face made of leaves, bursting from the verdant forest. Sometimes he is depicted as a playful, inviting figure, drumming up feelings of spring and joy. Other times he is a frightening figure, warning of the spirits from the old world that still haunt the woods. Though his cult following has diminished over the past several hundred years, they still live on in the May Day (Beltane) celebrations of today. While classically depicted as male presenting, this has definitely changed over time, mostly as artists take license with their own interpretation. Aside from a few fertility-related things that were later attributed to the Green Man, there is nothing that says the Green Man has any gender at all.

A Prayer to the Green Man

Verdant god of leaf and stem whose wisdom is the knowledge of the green world, I beseech you: come now from the hidden places; I welcome you into my home. Come now from beneath the canopy; I welcome you into my life. Bring with you the blessings of the wilds and keep safe the plants I grow. Bring with you a breath of freedom so that your spirit I will know.

The Others

The term *faerie* (fairy, fae) is used as a broad brush in contemporary times that can be synonymous with several other words—from god or demigod to sprite, depending on who you ask. By its very definition the term is vague and nebulous, and I would like to keep it that way. What we do know of the fae is that they are always connected to the wild, even those who choose to live amongst us, and they are liminal beings who tend to be both of our world and yet of another at the same time. There is also something distinctly magical about them, something that tends to make them attracted to magical people and magical places. In my experience it's common for witches to have faeries around them, even when they don't know it.

We can develop relationships with them, but in general faeries can be tricky to get ahold of or make partnerships with, especially those from the wildest places, which make up the majority. Those that are attracted to you will undoubtedly settle in your home and become part of what ultimately is a big spiritual ecosystem. We want this to happen, as they keep our homes safe and free of spiritual pests, acting as a sort of immune response—not as a function of service, but more as a function of their own preservation. Being magical beings, they also increase the magic energy (and I use that term in the most woo-woo way I can) in your household, making spells and practices all the more effective.

What I have noticed isn't so much that faerie spirits come riding in on my new houseplants, but rather that the ones who are already here really enjoy them. My inclination is that this has to do with the energy of the green flame, which I firmly believe is the life force for these beings. Our magic and psychic energy attracts them (which is enhanced by the plants), and the plants provide the perfect environment for them to thrive in. In return, their energy increases magical potency, and they keep your home free of unwanted energies.

If you do want to reach out to the faeries in your home, leave them an offering of tea or spirits (alcohol) at dusk and recite the following:

The Charge of the Fae

I bid the spirits from betwixt and between
Those of this world and of the unseen!
I know you are in this place that we share
For I am a witch who chooses to dare!
I leave you this offering as you have been shown
An act of friendship that should be known.

Your Gods

If you belong to a tradition or already work with a pantheon of deities from a specific cultural background, I highly recommend you make space in your life for whoever the divine vegetative spirit that is familiar to you might be. Who I have spoken about so far are those divine faces that I personally work with the most, but trust me when I tell you there are green gods coming out of every walk of life. Instead of giving you a list of deities, I will instead implore you to use Google if you are curious about the others I haven't brought to your attention. While I would love to dive into the stories of each individual green god, we have a lot of ground to cover, so I am going to leave the religious stuff to you. That being said, from one hortocculturist to the next, I think it is a good idea to work with plants as a bridge to every aspect of your spiritual life. If you have the opportunity and desire to work with a specific deity, then you should do it, but you do not need to in order to have a successful practice.

Green Gnosis

PART TWO

As I said before, for me, when it comes to the occult, everything circles back to working with spirits. Some of the most fortifying experiences I have had are with spirits related to the green flame. We are going to spend the next several chapters diving into ways we can cultivate a practice with these spirits, but there are a few things I would like to ask you before we move on. If you don't mind, get out that journal we talked about and respond to the following prompts. When you are finished, I will see you in the next chapter.

- *What plants do you have an existing connection to? When did you notice this connection, and when do you think it started?*
- *What type of houseplants do you enjoy the most? What about them do you find pleasing and why? Do you associate any emotions or experiences to them?*
- *What does the green flame feel like to you?*
- *Based on your experiences, what are areas in your houseplant care regimen that could benefit from guidance from your green guides?*
- *Describe your green guides.*
- *Who are Mother Nature and the Green Man to you, and what are ways that you can invite them into your practice?*
- *Lastly, are there any deities or spirits in traditions or pantheons you already follow who you might consider being part of your plant practice, such as those related to crops or forests?*

Chapter Three

The Green Name

In some Native languages the term for plants
translates to "those who take care of us."

. . .

Robin Wall Kimmerer, *Braiding Sweetgrass*

In witchcraft and occultism we often take on what we refer to as "magical names" that are generally used only within certain spaces. These names aren't just part of a secret identity that allows us to perform our workings with anonymity; they are also a way for us to align ourselves with greater powers and imbue our very lives with them. Some folks choose to take on multiple pseudonyms, while others pick one and stick with it for life. Some choose to use their names publicly, while others choose to keep them private. How you apply the name is up to you, but the *why* behind it is what I find valuable. Check out the bibliography and recommended reading for more resources about crafting a broader magical name that is right for you. For our purposes, however, we are going to talk about creating a magical name that can help enhance our connection to the green flame and the plants we care for.

I have had several magical names in my life; admittedly, not all of them have sounded cool. My first was "Blue Clover Moon," and while I enjoy clover, the moon, and the color blue, their powers combined definitely left me wanting more as I progressed along my path. Aside from those few super-secret names that I don't dare print, no name other than my given name ever seemed to fit very well—that is, until I crafted a magical name that I could work with when approaching the plant kingdom. Instead of going the traditional route of calling upon certain species and the moon as separate energies that I was pulling together, instead I asked myself a simple question: If I were a plant, what would my name be?

Friends, this is not the usual way one might go about these things, but I figured that if I wanted to be in Rome, I might as well do as the Romans do, so to speak. Let's take a look at botanical names and what exactly they mean. This will help us work better with the plants and plant spirits that we will be approaching as well as give us keen insight into how we might craft our own name.

Botanical Names

Each plant has a name that works as a sort of code that, if you know how to crack, can provide an almost endless amount of information about the plant. Within this information you will find clues about everything from its genetic heritage to the way its flowers are going to look! You can also use that botanical name to help summon the plant spirit by chanting their name over and over again before you begin working with a new specimen.

One of my favorite games to play is the "botanical name game" where I go around and rattle off the botanical (sometimes referred to as simply "Latin" or "horticultural") name of a plant. Interestingly enough, binomial names are not always written strictly in Latin; in fact, several contain elements of Greek or other languages, as you'll see in the following chart. It is common to see someone's name as part of a binomial name, as is the case with the genus *Schefflera*, which is named after the German physician Johann Peter Ernst von Scheffler. Because we use the Latin names for plants, it always sounds like I am summoning a spirit on a television show, and honestly that is half the fun! I realize, however, that this isn't everyone's cup of tea and that looking at the botanical name can be a little confusing, if not overwhelming, for some.

These names also have universal acceptance in the scientific and horticultural communities, which allows for a shared language to develop cross-culturally. The longer you are around plants, the more you will be looking at their botanical names and not their common or folk names.

Common names vary from region to region and are often applied to multiple plants so they aren't as reliable. Botanical names, however, are used across the globe and are what we have all decided would be our shared standard for communicating the vital information of a plant to one another.

Botanical names are derived from the same system used to classify all life on the planet and could technically consist of eight individual sections, representative of each level of taxonomic hierarchy. However, we only use the last two parts of the taxonomy to create what is referred to as a binomial name. It is the binomial name that you see on plant tags and in reference books.

The first part of the binomial name is the plant's genus. A genus is a grouping of plants that share a common ancestor and derive from the same family. Think of it like your last name. The second name is known as the epithet (or species) and is more like your first name. This is one of those areas where my occult brain really geeks out.

In ancient Greece and Rome, epithets were used to describe a specific aspect of a god's essence. Polias Athena is the aspect of Athena who protects the cities; she is a battle goddess as Promachos Athena and the granter of victory as Nike Athena. These are each versions of Athena—her light is always there; it merely shines with a different hue when it comes through in these forms. Like siblings, they are distinct from one another yet share the same source and carry the vibration of the original.

Thinking of epithets found in binomial nomenclature this way can help us immediately make a spiritual connection with the individual plant spirits related to them.

The name for the common houseplant known as devil's ivy or pothos is *Epipremnum aureum,* written as *E. aureum.* Aureum means yellow, referring to the yellow variegation that the foliage produces. That variegation, however, is a genetic mutation from the *Epipremnum* Schott (or true *Epipremnum*). The *Epipremnum pinnatum* is another mutation; however, instead of it being one of color, it is a mutation in leaf shape. When *E. pinnatum* mutated with a color variance, it gained the additional distinction of *variegata,* meaning variegated. The color of the variegation is usually (but not always) slipped in before the final epithet, so if *E. pinnatum* has a yellow variegated leaf, the botanical name for this new species would be *E. pinnatum aurea* (or *aureum*) *variegata.* If that leaf had white variegation, that would be referred to as *alba,* meaning white.

The epithet represents a version of the original plant, or a species of the genus, in the same way that an epithet in ancient Rome represents a version of a deity, or a face of the divine. If the genus is like your last name, the epithet is like your first. However, unlike the way we say names in the West, our first name would come after our last.

You don't need to become an expert in Latin to understand botanical names, but knowing these common terms will help you understand them better.

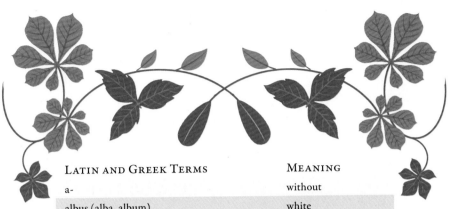

Latin and Greek Terms	Meaning
a-	without
albus (alba, album)	white
amphi-	on all sides
angustus (angustum, angusta)	narrow
arch- (archi-, archo-), -archus	ruler, highest
argenteus (argentatus, argentata, argentatum)	silvery
atropurpureus (atropurpurea, atropurpureum)	deep purple
aureus (aurea, aureum)	golden
auritus (auritus, aurita, auritum)	big eared, big leafed
australis (australe)	southern
baccatus (baccata, baccatum)	berry bearing
borealis (boreale)	northern
brachy- (also brevy-)	short
bulbus (bulbosus, bulbosa)	bulb
caeruleus (caerulea, caeruleum)	blue
caulos (acaulis, acaule)	stem, stalk
chloro-	pale green
chordatus (chordata, chordatum)	spined
-cola	inhabitant
coronatus (coronata, coronatum)	crowned
crassus, crassi- (crassa, crassum)	thick, fat
cristatus (cristata, cristatum)	crested
crypto-	hidden
digitatus (digitata, digitatum)	having fingers
dorsum (dors)	back

Latin and Greek Terms	Meaning
echinatus (echinata, echinatum)	prickly, spiny
edulis (edule)	edible
elegans (elegantissimus, elegantissima)	elegant
-ensis	from a place
erectus (erecta, erectum)	upright
erosus (erosa, erosum)	serrated, jagged
erythro-	red
esculentus (esculenta, esculentum)	edible
fallax	false
falx (falcatus, falcata, falcatum, falciformis)	sickle
familiaris	domestic, common
ferox	bold, ferocious
ferus (fera, ferum)	wild
folium	leaf
furcatus (furcata, furcatum)	forked
glandulosus (glandulosa, glandulosum)	having kernels
glutinosus (glutinosa, glutinosum)	sticky
gracilis (gracile)	slender
graveolens (gravis)	strong-smelling
hetero	different
homo	same, also humankind
hortensis (hortense)	of the garden
hybridus (hybridum, hybrida)	hybrid
hydro	water
hyper-	above, over

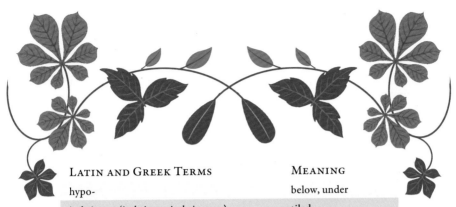

Latin and Greek Terms	Meaning
hypo-	below, under
imbricatus (imbricata, imbricatum)	tiled
inedulis (inedule)	inedible
ingratus (ingrata, ingratum)	offensive
lact-	milky, sappy
laetus (laetum)	pleasant, bright
lancea	lance
lateralis	side
limosus (limosa, limosum)	muddy
lineatus	striped
longi- (longus, longum, longa)	long
macro- (macra, macrum)	large
maculatus (maculata, maculatum)	spotted
marginatus (marginata, marginatum)	bordered
melano (melanus, melana)	black
micro-	small
minuta	small
mono-	single
morpho-	shape
nanos (nanus)	dwarf
niger (nigra, nigras, nigrus, nigrum, nigrescens)	black
nothos	false, wrong
nucifera	bearing nuts
obscurus (obscura, obscurum)	dark
occidentalis (occidentale)	western

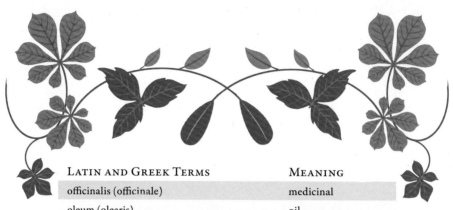

Latin and Greek Terms	Meaning
officinalis (officinale)	medicinal
oleum (olearis)	oil
-opsis	resembling
orientalis (orientale)	eastern
ovatus (ovata, ovatum)	egg-shaped
pallidus (pallida, pallidum)	pale
palustris (paluster, palustre, palustrium)	of the marsh
pan-	all
paradoxus (paradoxa, paradoxum)	uncharacteristic, unexpected
parilis (parile)	equal
parvus (parvum)	small
ped	foot
pholis	horny scale
phyllo	leaf
pictus (picta, pictum)	painted
platy	flat, broad
pod-	stem, foot, leg
poly-	many
pomum (pomifer, pomifera, pomonella)	fruit
praecox	early
prātum (pratensis, pratense, praticola)	meadow
princeps	leader
proto-	first
pruriens	itchy

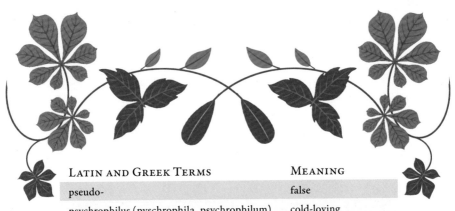

Latin and Greek Terms	Meaning
pseudo-	false
psychrophilus (pyschrophila, psychrophilum)	cold-loving
pungens	pungent
radix (radicans, radicatus, radicis, rhiza)	root
rāmus (ramosus, ramosa, ramulosus)	branch, branching
regalis (regale)	royal
repandus (repanda, repandum)	turned or curved upward
repens (reptans)	creeping, crawling
reticulata (reticulatum, reticulatus)	has interlacing lines
sanctus	sacred
sanguis (sanguinis)	blood
sativus (sativa, sativum)	cultivated
speciosus (speciosa, speciosum)	special, showy
sperma	seed
stoma	mouth, opening
striatus (striata, striatum)	striped
strictus (stricta, strictum)	tight
sulcatus (sulcata, sulcatum)	furrowed
tardus (tardi-)	late, slow
tenax	clinging, tough, tenacious
tenuis (tenue)	slender, fine, thin
terrestris (terrestre)	of the earth
tomentosus (tomentosa, tomentosum)	furry

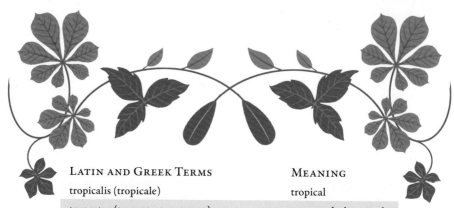

Latin and Greek Terms	Meaning
tropicalis (tropicale)	tropical
truncatus (truncata, truncatum)	truncated, shortened
ulos (ulo)	woolly
variabilis (variabile)	variable
variegatus (variegata, variegatum)	variegated
viridis (viride)	green
virosus (virosa)	poisonous

Isn't horticultural Latin fun? I mentioned earlier that you can chant the botanical name of a plant to help connect to its plant spirit. This is probably the easiest way, but it is certainly not the only way. Remember that it will take time for you to meet and build a rapport with most plant spirits. Some will most certainly pop out to you and want your attention; the spirit of your favorite plant has likely done that and is responsible in part for your connection. The majority, however, will need some sweetening up and a gentle touch.

Crafting Your Green Name

Inspired by botanical names and binomial nomenclature, we can craft a special green name just for you and your hortocculture. Now, we are talking about Latin here, so it is okay to fumble through this a bit. After you create the name, you might choose to use the whole thing or maybe just a part. It all works! And if one day you find that you somehow put the pieces of Latin together incorrectly, you can rest assured that is easy to fix. The good news—and the reason I feel confident in sharing this with you—is that we are creating a name, not stringing words together to form a sentence. I think you've got this!

The first place to start is going to be the genus name. Technically we belong to the genus *Homo,* with our species name being *sapiens*. But since we are trying to shed our current identity and step into one that is more verdant, we are going to pretend we are plants, not people. The genus name is representative of your family, environment, and background, so think about your roots and a botanical Latin term or word (from what I have provided or that you find on your own) that symbolizes those roots. In my case, being born in the Appalachian Mountains and being proud of my heritage, I might use *Appalachia*. Perhaps you are from the Americas and might choose *Americanus*. Maybe you're British and want to use the term *Brittanicus*. Perhaps your ancestors are a big deal in your life, so you use the word *Sanguine* (from *sanguinis*, meaning blood), or maybe you really like wine and want to celebrate that by taking the name *Baccatus* (meaning berry bearing). All of these are used in plant names!

I personally ended up choosing the name *Ferox*, meaning bold and ferocious. I feel that not only represents my family and my roots, as I am descended from a list of colorful characters, but also that it matches my vibe quite well.

The last part is your epithet. Remember, the epithet represents your unique personality and approach to life (and magic). Following the same procedure as before, think about what those characteristics are, or even what you want them to be, and draw a name from binomial nomenclature. I chose to go with two words: *argentata* (meaning silver) and *coronatum* (meaning crown). Altogether, my green name is *Ferox argentata coronatum*, but my plants and green friends just call me *Cor*. Okay, to be fair, this isn't my actual magical name, but it is close! Remember, some secrets we should always keep to ourselves.

What to Do with Your Green Name

Just as chanting the botanical name of a plant can help you connect with its indwelling spirit, chanting your own green name can help you connect with the green flame. I know this all sounds a bit silly from the outside, but from the inside we are further constructing a reality where the green flame and all its parts are real elements in our lives. For this to work, you should keep it secret and only share it among a select group of people, if at all. This helps keep it all personal and magical, free from outside spectacle or interference. Keep the name special because it is special; it represents you as well as your connection to the green flame.

Once you have a green name, the easiest way to start using it is to introduce yourself to your plants. The next time I watered them after taking a name, I reintroduced myself. To my surprise, I felt no more silly than I do when I am dancing alone in front of them. It did, however, start a process that I wish I had started sooner—one that has brought me closer to my plants on a spiritual level.

The next thing I did was to create a sigil for my green name. A sigil, for those who don't know, is a talismanic symbol created to represent a person, action, deed, or pretty much anything you can think of. Again, for a full run-through on creating sigils and all the possibilities that come with them, I am going to point you to my recommended reading section. There are other witches who have devoted entire books to the subject who could do a far better job than I am here of explaining them. But what I can do is give you a quick review of the easiest way to create a sigil that can be used for our purposes. As you travel through the last part of the book and explore each individual plant, I encourage you to create sigils of your own that correspond with the plant spirits you encounter. I apply the following method when doing so in my own practice.

Basic Sigil Making

My favorite method to employ for this requires you to have a piece of paper you can easily doodle on and something to draw with. I recommend a pencil with an eraser as you will likely find you will want to adjust the image as you move along. Here is a step-by-step guide using my green name as a template.

STEP ONE: Write out your green name (A) and then remove the vowels and any duplicate letters (B).

A: FEROX ARGENTATA CORONATUM

B: FRXGNTCM

STEP TWO: Using your own bit of creativity, stack and arrange the remaining letters so they combine to create a single image. It is perfectly acceptable to hide letters within letters; for example, G and C share a common shape and for our purposes can be combined easily. I can also add a small line to the letter T and blend both T and F together in that way. As long as you can look at the finished product and identify where those letters are, how you arrange them is totally up to you!

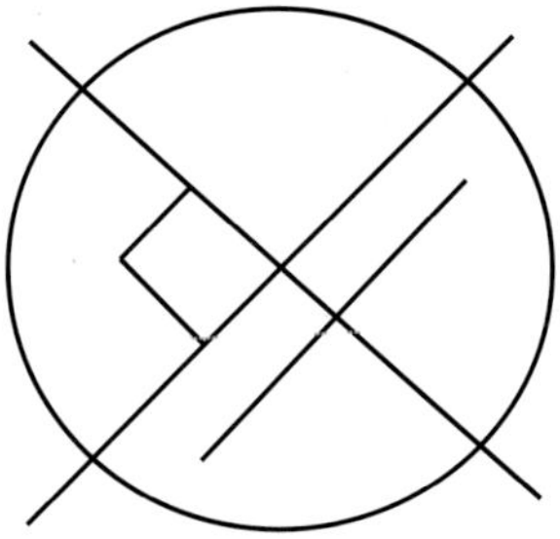

STEP THREE: To finish it all up, you then go in and embellish the symbol to stylize it and further hide the meaning from anyone who might see it other than yourself. After some doodling, this is what I eventually came up with.

Keep this symbol as secure as your name; both can serve to take you further in this practice than you could ever imagine. Our next topic is going to show you a few ways this is possible.

Green Gnosis

PART THREE

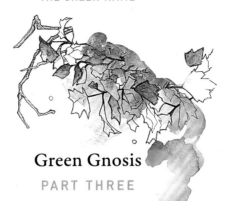

If you haven't already, take out that handy-dandy journal of yours and jot down your sigil notes, an explanation of what it means to you, and of course a drawing of the sigil itself. Think back to chapter 1, when we discussed the three words that distilled our understanding of what the green flame was and felt like. In the example, mine were "pervasive, verdant, life." Using your three words, create a sigil that represents the green flame to you by applying the same method discussed in this chapter.

Next, choose up to three of your houseplants and, using their binomial name, create a sigil that represents each of those plants to you.

Chapter Four

Magical Plant Care

> Connection with gardens, even small ones, even potted plants, can become windows to the inner life. The simple act of stopping and looking at the beauty around us can be prayer.
>
> • • •
>
> Patricia R. Barrett, *The Sacred Garden*

Any plant can be a houseplant; you merely have to provide the right environment for it to grow in. That doesn't mean that every plant *should* be a houseplant, however, as I am a firm believer that most plants belong in their natural setting, but in my time as a houseplant hortocculturist I have learned that where there is a will, there is a way. While I don't have space to get into all the specifics of raising a prize-winning rare orchid, this chapter is dedicated to sharing everything you need to know to successfully care for your magical houseplants by creating the perfect environment for them.

For me, caring for my houseplants is an act of devotion just as much as it is an essential part of owning them. I do my best to approach it with reverence and intention; when I am caring for my plants, I take the time to connect to them and make sure they are getting what they need. It is also a good time to put my headphones on, listen to music that makes me happy, and dance all around the house. When I do this, I am not just dancing to let loose and have some fun; I am doing it as an act of service. The plants know I am dancing for them—and between you and me, I think they like it. Plant care can be as spiritual or monotonous as you make it.

In this chapter we are going to discuss plant care as both a need-to-know element of hortocculture and a path to devotion.

There are a lot of misconceptions about how to raise indoor plants. Most often these misconceptions come from the belief that there is a one-size-fits-all option for how plants should be cared for, but the truth is far from this belief. Plants respond differently to different environmental factors, and what works for someone in one part of the world might not work for someone in another. Furthermore, what works for someone on the bottom floor of an apartment building with southern exposure likely won't work for someone on the third floor of the same building with eastern exposure. Yes, that means you could get a plant, read the information card and do everything right according to it, and still end up killing it because it wasn't properly cared for. In my experience, where people tend to go wrong with caring for their plants is that they are following the wrong rules for their home environment.

There is also a difference between a plant that is growing and a plant that is thriving. For those houseplants we work with in magic, we want them to be as strong and full of life force as possible. So even if you are an old pro and have a house full of plants, there still might be room for improvement. I learn new plant hacks every day!

Lighting

This is one of the more deceptive aspects of growing plants because the terms used to describe the amount of light a plant should receive are sometimes misleading. Most houseplants want "bright indirect light"—but what exactly does that even mean? There are, of course, very technical specifications for what constitutes medium or high light and everything in between; however, the average person does not have the equipment to test the quality of light their plants are receiving. Instead of worrying about the technical specifications, on the following spread is a visual map of a north-facing room at high noon when the sun is at its highest. Use this as a reference to help you figure out where to place plants in your own home.

In general, if a beam of sunlight is touching the leaves, it is receiving direct sunlight. If it is near a sunbeam but not being touched directly by the beam, it is in "bright indirect light." The farther you move away from the direct sunbeam, the lower the quality of light. Lighting is not too difficult to sort out when you think of it like this.

The problem, however, is that we don't always have right light for the plant, and we will need to provide a secondary light source, also known as a grow light. Not all grow lights are equal! We can spend hours talking about which grow lights work best, and out of all the investments I have made to support what I lovingly refer to as my "plant habit," grow lights are on the top of the list. Let me save you valuable time, effort, and money, friend!

Grow Light Specifications

The type of grow light you need for your plants depends on the size of the job. It is safe to say that the bigger a plant or the more plants you need to light in one area, more light will be required, which can mean you either need a big light or perhaps multiple smaller lights. But there are also other factors besides size and

A NORTH-FACING ROOM AT HIGH NOON SHOWS PLANTS BY WINDOW IN BRIGHT INDIRECT LIGHT, PLANTS TO IMMEDIATE SIDES OF WINDOW ARE IN MEDIUM LIGHT, AND PLANTS ON SIDES OF ROOM ARE IN LOW LIGHT

number of lights to consider, such as color, wattage, output, and positioning. Let's look at factors you should consider when purchasing and setting up lights. Keep in mind that houseplants should get between twelve and sixteen hours of artificial light each day. You do not need to adjust this per season.

Color

Plants require the right wavelengths of light to undergo photosynthesis, and most indoor lighting doesn't provide this. Full spectrum means that the light will contain all necessary wavelengths required for plant growth (like the sun does). This is essentially what makes a grow light a grow light; it can provide a spectrum of light comparable to natural sunlight.

While I am lucky to have some fantastic natural lighting in my home, I also have to artificially light much of it to accommodate for the plant collection. In my office I have very little natural light, so it is entirely lit by grow lights.

Fun fact: If you want to avoid your home looking like a laboratory, go with the yellow variety of light over the white as it looks closer to natural lighting.

You will also see pink/purple LED lights on the market, which are lights that achieve their full spectrum capability by using red, blue, and sometimes white lights simultaneously. This causes the light emitted to appear pink or violet, depending on the desired outcome. Red light wavelengths are known to have the highest efficacy when transferring electricity into light, meaning little energy is lost in the process. More importantly, however, is that plants love red light because its energy is almost immediately available for photosynthesis. Blue and white lights are used to bring a bit of balance to the spectrum.

I work with both full spectrum yellow lights and pink lights and have had success with both. I personally find that the darker houseplants benefit the most from pink lights, and I think this might have to do with bleaching caused over time by the full spectrum. While yes, pink lights do provide more immediate energy for the plants, it does make spotting problems with your plants more difficult and can be a bit too much over time. Ultimately, however, it is your personal choice.

From there, you will need to determine its output, which will depend on how much space you need to cover.

Wattage, Output, and Positioning

When working with fluorescent lights, you want nothing less than what is called a full spectrum T5 grow light. "T" in lamp nomenclature represents the shape of a lamp, and the number represents the diameter of the lamp in eighths of an inch. So, a T5 lamp has a diameter of five-eighths of an inch. Any plant that is directly under your average T5 grow light will be receiving bright indirect light. These are going to be long two-foot rods that will require special mounting. I hang mine from the ceiling with chains. Fluorescent lights produce a lot of ambient heat, meaning they make your space hot and lose a lot of energy, which isn't good for the electric bill. While these are totally fine to work with, there is a safer and more energy efficient way to grow: use LED lights.

I also recommend using LED lights for a couple of reasons, the first being that they have a much longer lifespan than fluorescent lights and therefore produce less waste. LED bulbs also produce much less heat than others. A few lamps can really heat up a room, so I take steps wherever I can to reduce that. Lastly, LED lights require way less energy. This is not only good for the environment but also for the electricity bill!

For many complicated reasons, wattage means very little in the world of LED grow lights. Their efficiency and construction have more to do with how well they perform, and different designs might use energy differently, say with a small internal fan or an updated design. So we are left to the manufacturers to tell us how useful their lights are. For this reason, I often use "T5 LED grow light" in my searches when looking for the right fit. This way, you can find light bulbs with the right output for your sexy plant corner or buy a LED bar system that divides the energy among a set of multiple lights so you can mount them to your shelves and grow plants that require less space.

While looking at the manufacturer's suggestions, be sure to look at how close the light will need to be to the plant in order to receive the best quality of light. Believe it or not, closer to the light isn't necessarily equivalent to more energy for the plant. Also, don't forget that some plants, like seedlings, do not usually do well under high amounts of indirect light. For more on plant lights as well as specific recommendations, check out my website ModernWitch.com.

Sigils for Grow Lights

As mentioned, I have a lot of artificial lighting in the house for my plants, and over time I realized that I was wasting a lot of potential magical energy by not incorporating them into my practice as well. After some trial and error, I discovered the best way to do that was to place sigils on them so that my plants are infused with magic from their light source. Here are seven sigils that I use regularly. Draw them directly on the lamp with a marker.

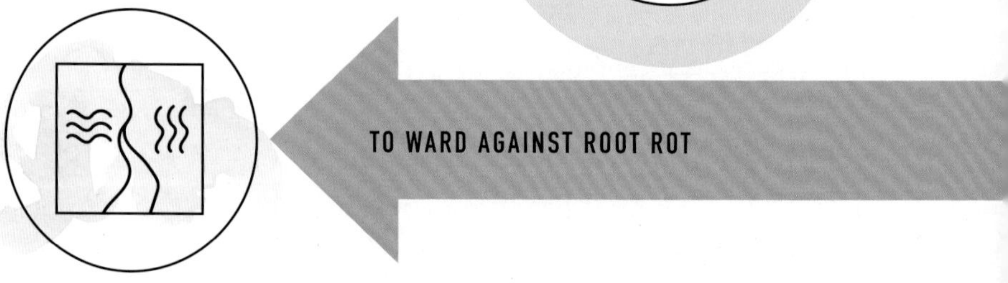

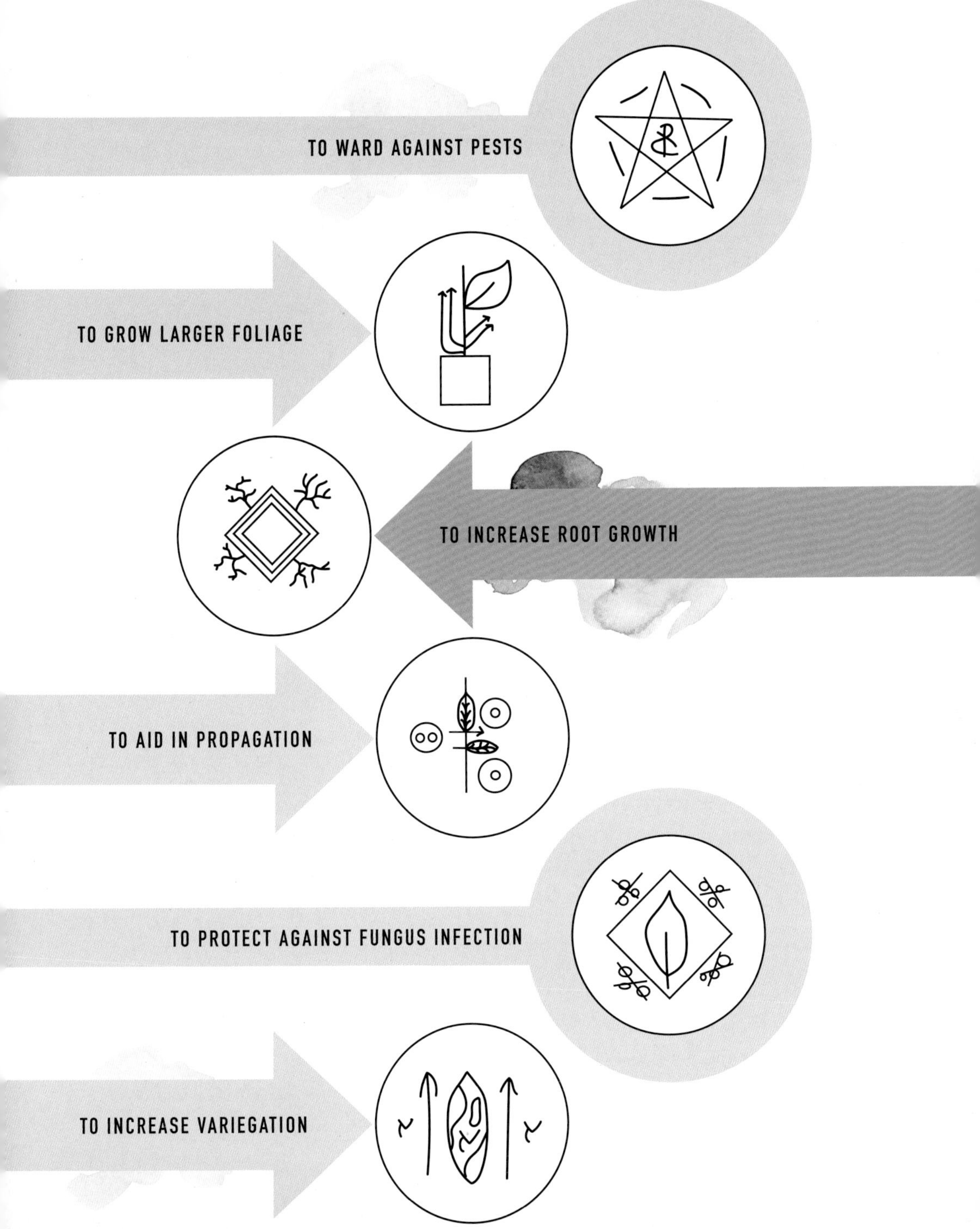
TO WARD AGAINST PESTS
TO GROW LARGER FOLIAGE
TO INCREASE ROOT GROWTH
TO AID IN PROPAGATION
TO PROTECT AGAINST FUNGUS INFECTION
TO INCREASE VARIEGATION

Temperature and Humidity

Temperature is important but not something you need to necessarily obsess over. Think about it like this: if you're cold, your plants are cold. Some plants don't mind this one bit, but some—like tropicals—very much do! Optimal temperature for growth depends on the individual species, but in general a temperature between 60 and 80°F is ideal.

The average home floats anywhere from between 30 and 60 percent humidity, depending on region. Experts tell us that ideally our homes should be around 45 percent humidity. The average houseplant is absolutely comfortable at around 45 percent, so if you maintain that normal recommended standard, your plants will likely be just fine unless they have special requirements. If you run an air conditioner or heater, you are most certainly stripping humidity out of the air, however, and will need to find ways of offsetting the dip created.

There are a few reasons why humidity matters, and most notable of those is that leaves are porous and will dry out if the air is too dry. New leaves will also have a more difficult time unfurling because moisture in the air acts as a natural lubricant. The soil will also dry out faster, which can lead to a whole other set of problems that we will discuss next.

You can increase humidity by placing shallow dishes full of rocks and water under your pots. The trick is to not submerge the bottom of the pot in water, but rather to place it so that the bottom of the pot is just above the waterline. The water evaporates under the pot and rises to bring moisture to the leaves without adding moisture to the substrate. This works best when plants are clumped together in one area. In an open setting with one or two plants, most of the evaporated water is going to be lost to natural air flow.

In spaces with open and moving air, I recommend a cool-mist humidifier. There are several affordable options, just be sure to avoid the warm humidifiers that essentially push out steam vapor as the heat can cause damage to leaves and promote bacteria.

Misting with a water bottle works well for an hour or two, but again, most of the moisture is lost to freely moving air. So, if you are going to solely rely on misting, you will likely want to do it more than once a day.

I like to keep crystals in my humidifiers. I do this for the same reason I put sigils on my grow lights: to further imbue the plants with magical energy and support. In particular, I like to use fluorite, Herkimer diamond, citrine, and Lemurian quartz. Each are excellent at cleansing and purifying energy as well as supporting magical processes.

Terrarium Shrines

Additionally, you can build a high-humidity environment like a terrarium, which is specifically designed to keep the immediate surrounding of the plant in above average humidity. There are open and closed methods that allow for more control. Because they are enclosed ecosystems that feel like their own little world, I started to turn my terrariums into shrines to spirits and gods that I work with. Each are themed and have statues or stones that work as little idols for the shrines. Instead of lighting incense for the spirits therein, which would be customary for a shrine, I mist them instead.

To build a terrarium shrine, you will need a container with a lid, preferably glass. You can also make an open terrarium shrine using a fishbowl or something similar. After cleaning it out with fresh water to make sure there is no residual chemical residue from soap, layer pebbles or perlite to fill the container approximately one-sixth of the way up. This will create a reservoir for water.

Next, put a layer of sphagnum moss that just covers the top of the pebbles or perlite, and then on top of that add dirt so that the container is one-third to one-half full.

Decorate and plant your terrarium however you like. I like to add painted stones with sigils on them representing the deity or spirit, and I work with plants that will remain small. There are several species of hoya, begonia, episcia, philodendron, and even ficus that thrive in these conditions. When you are ready, water it evenly until the reservoir is full. The sphagnum moss will wick the water from the perlite up to the soil and keep your plant's roots happy.

Occasionally mold will spring up in a terrarium, and that is never fun. To solve this problem without harsh chemicals, I brew a strong tea made from chamomile, which has a compound that kills mold. Mist the mold directly twice a day until it is gone, which usually happens between 24 and 48 hours.

Water

One of the biggest places where people tend to mess up with plant care is with watering. I struggle with this all the time, and so does every plant person I know. This is because every plant goes through water at a different rate depending on how fast it is growing, what substrate it is in, and how humid its environment is.

As you might imagine, in a more humid environment water doesn't evaporate as quickly, which means it is easier to overwater your plants—especially since a lot of plants that require high humidity do not like to have very wet roots. Both overwatering and underwatering can can lead to a lot of bad stuff, so let's go over the essentials.

What it means to overwater one plant means something very different to another, so be sure to check out the info on your plant when you get it. Some plants, like *Colocasia* and ferns, very much love to be sitting in water at almost all times. Spider plants and calathea want moist but not soggy soil. Succulents and cacti want to be in dry conditions most of the time. What is underwatering to the *Colocasia* would be perfect for the calathea but detrimental to a cactus.

The finer and loamier the soil, the more water is retained and the risk of overwatering increases in normal humidity. The chunkier the soil, the less water it retains and the easier it is to dry out in normal humidity. If you find that you are an overwaterer, then amending the soil so it is more chunky by adding perlite and bark will help with over-retention. Likewise, if you underwater, then adding loamy soil to your mix will help to bring the right balance.

Overwatering causes the buildup of bacteria that causes what we call root rot. Root rot is when the root of the plant becomes waterlogged and dies. When this happens, it spreads quickly and you can easily lose the entire root system, if not large chunks of it. This cannot be remedied once it has happened; instead, you have to cut off the dead root and wait for the plant to regrow those lost roots.

Constant underwatering causes dry rot, which is where the root dries up and dies. Once the root dies and you water the plant, that dead root can become waterlogged, which can result in root rot!

How do you know if you're incorrectly watering? Classic signs of overwatering include yellow edges on lower leaves, the entire plant wilting when soil is wet, no new growth, and even algae growth on the top of the soil. Classic signs that you are underwatering are the plant wilting if soil is dry, drying/crispy leaves, and slow growth.

The best standard to keep is that most plants like for their soil to dry out, but not completely, before being thoroughly watered. Here's why: as the soil dries, the roots grow to essentially follow the water. By allowing the top one or two inches of the soil to dry you are ensuring that the root can grow and avoid being waterlogged. To check this, just stick your finger in the pot and give it a wiggle. If the top 1–2 inches feel dry, then you know it is time!

There are a few methods for telling how dry the soil might be, but I am old school and suggest just sticking your finger in it. Go down an inch or two and see how it feels. Does it feel dry? How much of it feels dry? You can also buy a soil moisture meter that can give you specific information, but I think sticking your finger in it is just fine.

A Note about Pots and Water

Keep in mind that all pots are not created equal when it comes to moisture control. Terra-cotta pots will wick water from the substrate, causing it to dry out faster. This is good for plants that like it on the drier side such as succulents and cacti, where water retention in the substrate can be a problem. Ceramic pots are glazed and not as porous, if at all, and don't wick water, keeping the substrate moist longer. The downside to using both terra-cotta and ceramic pots that are not glazed on the inside is that their porousness makes them breeding grounds for bacteria and the ideal place for fungus and some pests. If you reuse that pot, you can very easily spread those issues to the next plant if it is not thoroughly cleaned and sanitized. If you have a large collection and are continually reusing your pots, I recommend using plastic for all practical purposes and ceramic for vanity purposes.

Plastic pots increase moisture retention, are inexpensive, and you can find them made from recycled materials. I stick my plastic pots inside my ceramic pots so I can still get the sexy look but have the reliability and versatility of plastic. I use clear plastic liners for my anthuriums, orchids, and hoyas, which allows me to check root health instantly without disturbing them. This is ideal for epiphytic plants whose roots are also capable of some degree of photosynthesis.

Sacred Waters

I tend to use liquid fertilizer and mix it in big 5-gallon barrels. Before adding the nutrients, I like to put charged crystals that are empowered to assist in plant growth in the barrel and place it in the sun so I can make a giant crystal elixir to water my plants with. My favorite combination of stones for this is citrine (the power of the sun), epidote (the power of the green flame), and black tourmaline (for banishing pests).

Additionally, I water the plants I work with for magic with moon water whenever I get the chance. Moon water is water that has been charged by the full moon and is said to carry its properties. To make it, all you need to do is put your water in a clear container and place that directly in the moonlight overnight. The next morning you have moon water!

Pest Control

The last little bit of care advice to get into for now is the controlling of pests on our houseplants. Friend, let me be honest: it is inevitable and can be quite discouraging. Bugs kinda just come with the territory as there are pests that have specifically evolved to take advantage of your plants. If not caught in time, an infestation can mean the end of your baby and possibly your entire collection.

The most common pests we will deal with when it comes to houseplants are the following:

SPIDER MITES feed off the sugars produced by the plant and usually live on the underside of leaves in protective webs they spin. They are very small and hard to see, often going unnoticed until they have reached maturity.

MEALYBUGS are a soft-bodied form of scale insect that look like white cottony masses that usually show up on new growth. They don't cause a lot of damage unless they are en masse; however, they excrete a substance called "honeydew" that can cause the growth of molds. Interestingly enough, ants are known to cultivate mealybugs (and other scale insects) to farm this honeydew as they feed off of it. It is not uncommon to see ants moving mealybugs between plants to establish new colonies for farming.

SCALE is a hard bodied insect that is related to mealybugs, which also produces honeydew and has a similar relationship to ants. Unlike mealybugs, male scale insects tend to have legs and wings and can fly from plant to plant before settling down to mate or feed. Females usually have legs and then lose them once they begin feeding. Scale insects (of which there are over 8,000 identified species) are known to be hermaphroditic, and some reproduce through parthenogenesis. Scale insects are unique in that once they begin feeding, they grow waxy shells that look like little scales, where they will remain until it is time to reproduce, which is shortly followed by death.

THRIPS are tiny, winged insects that feed off of plants and can quickly destroy whatever they are infesting. They are one of the more difficult pests to treat as their ability to fly means they can hide easily. They have been known to also bite humans and animals in search of moisture, which can cause skin irritation.

GNATS/FRUIT FLIES are tiny flies that love to lay eggs in plant soil. They feed off of naturally occurring fungus and even though an adult has only a week-long lifespan, it can lay up to one hundred and fifty eggs, which only take a few days to hatch. They don't cause harm to your plants, but they can be incredibly annoying and can get out of control easily. They can come in on fruit from the supermarket or in the soil of a new plant.

The good news is, there is plenty that can be done about them both organically and inorganically.

If doing things organically is important to you, then you aren't alone. Many houseplant enthusiasts demand organic treatment in their homes because of immediate environmental concerns. There are three primary methods for taking care of pests organically, all of which can be used offensively as well as for treatment.

SOAPY WATER works wonders, especially the special liquid soap that you can procure called "insecticidal soap," which contains natural ingredients that can kill soft-bodied predators but mostly make the leaves inedible. I spray this whenever I water as part of my plant care regimen. It doesn't make the plant sticky or even leave much of a film, but it does work well as an offensive measure. When I am treating a plant that has an infestation, however, I spray the leaves down and then gently scrub the leaf with a makeup brush to disturb any nests. Pests like spider mites are super tiny and are often unnoticed until they have already established themselves and start building webs. Simply spraying won't kill their eggs or babies living in the nests, so you have to disturb them to ensure total coverage. If a leaf is yellowing or dead, remove it immediately.

NEEM OIL is an all-natural pesticide that kills most houseplant pests. It is extracted from the neem plant and has a unique, almost garlicy capsicum-like scent that is an acquired taste. Neem oil products are

TO MAKE A SOAPY SPRAY, MIX ONE TABLESPOON OF UNSCENTED DISH, CASTILE, OR INSECTICIDAL SOAP WITH ONE QUART OF WATER.

becoming quite popular; however, the average treatment involves mixing two tablespoons of neem oil in one gallon of water and then spraying.

The other natural treatment method is to use BENEFICIAL PREDATORY INSECTS AND NEMATODES. Now, you may not be keen on releasing even more bugs into your home, but some people don't mind at all. In my plant room I release ladybugs to help keep the pest population down. Ladybugs and green lacewing larvae are frequently used for this purpose because they eat the bugs that are eating your plants. You can buy ladybugs in the spring and summer at most hardware stores and online. Lacewings are available from breeders throughout the year, depending on location.

Beneficial nematodes, on the other hand, are added to soil because they seek out and eat the larval forms of pests. They are perfectly harmless (unless you are a pest) and only live for a few weeks.

Then there are the INORGANIC PESTICIDES. I tried for years to avoid them, but once the collection got to a certain size, organic measures didn't seem to cut it. After doing a lot of research, I eventually came to the conclusion that systemic pesticides were the best way to go. Systemic pesticides treat the soil in an effort to stop the problem where it begins. The poison is then drunk by the plants and delivered to the insect. Most systemic treatments don't kill the insect but rather make the plant inedible. There are several options available out there. I recommend seeing which is the right one for your home. What I like about the systemic treatment is that when I use it, my need for spraying goes way down. I might see one or two mealybugs, but that is about it. It doesn't work instantly, however; rather, the results produce themselves over time.

Finally we get to how to tackle FUNGUS GNATS. Outside of nematodes, organic treatments never worked for this problem. Instead, I found a product known as "Mosquito Bits" that you add to the soil, which releases a chemical that kills mosquito and gnat larvae. There are a few brands that sell this product, and it is easy to find at most hardware stores. This is ideal because it keeps them from maturing to adulthood, where they will end up laying even more eggs.

Trimming and Caring for Foliage

Leaves die off all the time; it is part of the natural growth process for many plants. Sometimes an accident happens, and the plant drops a few leaves or the variegated part of a plant turns brown and starts to look unseemly. Not only do you want to tend to the plant to keep it healthy, but you also want to make sure it looks presentable; after all, it is part of your home décor. No one wants a withering plant in a corner.

To keep your plants looking and being healthy, you will need to trim brown spots and cut off dying leaves as they begin to fade. Pests love to hide on these places, which can further spread the problem to other plants, and bacteria and fungus thrive on decaying plant tissue. Removing them when you see them is a necessary part of keeping your plants happy. If you are removing leaves that have been affected by pests or fungus, you do not want to compost them once they are removed as this can spread the problem. Instead, throw them in the trash and then remove the trash from your home once you are done cleaning up.

On thicker leaves like those of a philodendron or anthurium, you can trim off browning areas to preserve the rest of the leaf. To do this, trim around the affected tissue, moving into the healthy part of the leaf by about a quarter of an inch. Cutting into the healthy portion will create a clean cut that the plant will be able to seal off, and it will stop rot from spreading. Be sure to do this with a pair of sterilized trimmers or scissors.

You will want to give your plants a shower once a month! In nature plants are subjected to rain and wind that help keep them clean and their pores free of dust and debris. If you want a healthy and vibrant plant, rinse off its leaves once a month. This is also an awesome way to reduce pests as keeping leaves clean makes the plant less hospitable to their needs.

Repotting

We have to repot our plants when they get too big for their current pots (also known as "up potting") or when we need to treat the roots and/or soil. Otherwise, we shouldn't be messing with the roots. They are much more sensitive than any other part of the plant, and repotting them unnecessarily can cause them to die back.

When up potting it is generally a good idea to increase by one to two pot sizes each time, depending on the plant. If you up pot into too big of a container, you run the risk of water not cycling through the pot fast enough and getting root rot.

When you do up pot, take advantage of the moment and recharge (or freshen up) the crystals and charms with fresh ones to keep your spells working flawlessly.

Propagation

To propagate a houseplant means to create more plants by cuttings, seeds, or even root division. There are other ways, but those are the main three you will likely run into. Propagating is a good thing; it means that your plants are strong and healthy, and the time has come for them to divide themselves up to form more plants.

There are a number of reasons we might choose to propagate a plant. The first and most common for houseplants is that the plant simply grew too big for its environment—not a problem in the wild but definitely a problem in a small room. The plant might have been attacked by pests and the only way to save it is to chop it up and propagate the nodes, which is an ingenious method to prolong the life of a beloved ally. Sometimes propagation happens naturally through the creation of seed and is part of the plant's lifecycle. Whatever the reason and whether or not you are an active participant in the process is up to you, but knowing how to propagate your plants is an important part of the care process. Let's take a look at the three techniques I mentioned and how to do them.

Cuttings (Cloning)

It may surprise you, but few houseplants on the market were grown from seed. They most likely are the product of cloning or tissue culture, which is a more extreme form of cloning. We call it cloning because we are taking tissue from a mother plant and using it to start the life of a new plant. There is no pollination or seed dispersal involved, and while technically the daughter plant is a separate plant from the mother, genetically they are identical.

Fun fact: Some plants, like the common pothos, are no longer capable of producing flowers because they were cloned from an immature specimen that had not yet developed the genetic fortitude to flower.

At the very least, I recommend taking what we refer to as an "insurance leaf," which is a leaf cutting that you have propagated so that if the mother plant were to fail for any reason, you have a second plant. Insurance leaves have saved my collection more than once! This will become more important the rarer the plant gets.

Every cutting must have a piece of leaf, stem, and node. Most plants such as philodendron, monstera, anthurium, syngonium, and epipremnum should be propagated this way. Trim off excess stem—I generally try to keep stems to about an inch in length on either side of the node. Be aware that some plants will start oozing out sap that might be toxic, so be sure to wear gloves.

Once you have taken your cuttings, allow them to air dry and callous over for a few hours before moving on. Many people prefer to dab the exposed areas with powdered cinnamon, which helps form the callous and prevents mold. This is only necessary if you are not planning on propagating them directly in water.

At this point you basically have three options on how to move forward. The first is to put it in a container with fresh water and change the water out every three days. It is important to change the water out as that allows for fresh oxygen to become available to the newly forming roots. You can also put a cutting from the average pothos in the water to help get the other cutting to root. There is a hormone produced by the pothos that can be supplemental for the cutting you are trying to root. New roots should form within one to three weeks. Once you see the formation of secondary roots, it is safe to plant in a substrate.

You can put the cutting into moist sphagnum moss and store within a clear plastic container that you place under a grow light or near a window to act as a terrarium. We call this a "prop box," and it is, in my opinion, the most effective way of rooting a cutting. Again, once you see the formation of secondary roots, it is safe to plant.

The other method is to place the stem cutting into seed-starting potting mix and then put it into a terrarium or a plastic bag that is propped up with sticks so it doesn't fall onto the plant. It is important for humidity to not be a concern for the new plant, so keeping it high and in terrarium conditions will take a lot of stress from its shoulders. You can tell new roots are forming when you have fresh growth coming from the soil. I wait until the third leaf emerges before I take it out of the terrarium conditions. Water when the soil is half dry, but do not allow it to sit in water.

There are a few genuses, such as begonia and peperomia, whose leaves can be propagated from a single leaf. In these cases, cut the stem up to about half an inch from the base of the leaf. Plant the leaf in seed-starting potting mix until only about two-thirds of the leaf is exposed. Place in a terrarium setting and water when the soil is half dry, but do not allow it to sit in water. You should have new leaves in two to four weeks.

Root Division

Some plants—such as alocasia, silver squill, and aglaonema—produce clones of themselves by forming corms under the surface of the soil that sprout into new plants. These are easily divided when repotting as they will form into new plants that separate from the mother plant on their own; if they are connected, they may be easily cut or broken off. As soon as you have the new plant, it is safe to put in soil.

Triage

Our next plant care topic involves how to rescue a dying plant. This is something that you will get better at with time and experience, but there are never any guarantees. Sometimes the plant is set on dying and there is nothing you can do to stop it. If you run into a situation where a plant you love is dying and you want to try and save it, there are only a small handful of things you can do. Here are the three most common things that go wrong with houseplants and how to fix them.

ROOT ROT happens when the roots are sitting in too much water for too long. It is the number one killer of houseplants because it is easy to overwater. Remove the plant from substrate and rinse the roots as thoroughly as you can. Cut back any dead growth from both the stem and the root system. Finding which roots are dead is easy as they will be mushy. Next, place the plant in new substrate or in sphagnum if it is particularly bad and you are working with only a small amount of stem and root. Water the substrate lightly, only allowing it to get about halfway wet, and then place the container in a terrarium environment in high indirect light. It may take a few weeks to a few months depending on the plant and time of year, but as long as the stem doesn't turn mushy, new growth should emerge.

You can just as easily NEGLECT A PLANT and forget to water it. In this case, cut back all the dead growth, water it thoroughly, and then place under bright indirect light. Water it again when it dries out one-third of the way to ensure you don't overwater it and cause the already damaged roots to rot. Usually fixing this issue is much faster than root rot, so you should expect new leaves within a few days to a couple of weeks depending on the season.

The third most common issue is that plants succumb to PEST INFESTATION. This is never fun but happens more often than many of us would care to admit. Treat this problem by cutting back all affected growth that is failing. Remove the plant from the substrate and rinse the entire plant thoroughly, being sure to gently rub any remaining leaves to remove pests and their eggs. Throw the soil out as it likely has pest larvae and eggs, and reusing it would prolong the issue. Spray the entire plant down with an insecticidal soap and then repot. Treat the plant every other day for the next three weeks by rinsing off the leaves and reapplying insecticidal soap. Repetition is key for this to work.

Understanding What Your Plant Needs

As I have already said, there is no one-size-fits-all approach to indoor plant care, but there is so much that we can learn in this regard by understanding the type of plant we are caring for. What I mean by this is that some plants like it drier than others, some want heavy fertilizers while others can't take even the tiniest amount, and some will remain mostly free of pests while others are going to be magnets for it. Understanding all of this going into the game is the only way to keep scoring points!

So, yes, any plant can be a houseplant, and I think you should safely grow whatever your witchy heart desires in your own home, but the term "houseplant" usually refers to subtropical species that have adapted to living in temperatures that are surprisingly close to our own comfort levels (60–80°F). These plants don't need to undergo dormancy or die after a growth season but rather can continue to grow as long as their conditions remain stable. Aside from the kitchen herb box, we don't usually consider annuals and perennials to be houseplants.

You will find that your regimen for plant care will grow to reflect the individual habits and needs of your plants. I have a few in my collection that seem to break the conventional rules, and I let them tell me what they need. Schedules are excellent, but don't get too reliant on them. The moment I get too comfortable with a plant care schedule, my plants start to do things to make me break that schedule. Instead, I have two days where I make sure to water if the plant needs, but I try to regularly check in with the plants as well. Are they drinking more water than they used to? Are they sitting in too much water? Do they have bugs? It is easy to just treat plant care as a chore, but really it should be thought of as an opportunity to check in with your friend.

Raising Indoor Plants with a Magical Mindset

It may sound like a bit of a no-brainer, but the most important thing you can bring to your magical plant care regimen is magic—*your* magic! Obviously, the whole reason for writing this book is to explore the topic of magical plant care and stewardship, but you have to remain committed to the process. Once you accept the mere idea that your plants are magical and full of psychic energy, you can't choose to one day ignore that gnosis. You must remain dedicated to it and to them. This means that your plants should be a constant part of your magical reality, not just when it is convenient.

Talk to them, surround yourself with them when you cast spells, hide your amulets and talismans in their foliage and inside their pots, learn to listen and grow alongside them. Even if you aren't actively engaging with your indoor plants in a working, remember that they are ever-present members of your magical team!

An excellent way to incorporate your existing magical practice with your houseplants is to follow the moon in your care regimen. This by no means is new news, but a lot of houseplant people don't consider the age-old wisdom that farmers have shared with us—plants are actually members of a lunar cult. Just kidding (but only a little).

Gardening by the Moon and Stars

The idea that the moon has an effect over plant growth may sound like superstition, but those ancient farmers were on to something. In fact, today—here in the US—you can pick up a farmer's almanac that will share information about gardening based on a lunar schedule that is still used today as the standard for most farmers and gardeners.

Moon Phases

According to agricultural tradition that goes all the way back to before the time of Pliny the Elder, an ancient Roman historian who wrote at length about the topic in his book *History of Nature, Vol 18*, the theory is that the moon affects the movement of fluid in plants similarly to how it affects the tides.

- » During the waxing moon, it is a good time to plant, sow, and take cuttings.
- » During the full moon, you should do all of those plus harvest fruits as they will be at their juiciest.
- » During the waning moon, you should weed and fertilize.
- » During the new moon, you should rest.

Moon Signs and Best Days

Another approach, often referred to as "best days," involves incorporating the astrological influences of the zodiac as the moon travels through each sign. Here we do not rely on the moon phase but rather its position in the heavens.

- » When the moon travels through Cancer, Scorpio, Pisces, or Taurus, it is a good time to plant, transplant, and graft.
- » When it travels through Aries, Leo, Sagittarius, Gemini, or Aquarius, it is safe to harvest, plow, control pests, and control weeds. It is also a good time to propagate plants and banish pests.
- » Pruning should be done when the moon is in a fire sign such as Aries, Leo, or Sagittarius.
- » Last, the building and mending of fences, as well as the preparation of garden beds, soils and substrates, and pots, should be done when the moon is in Capricorn.

In addition to helping us get insight into when we might perform an act like taking a cutting for a magical spell or when would be best to transplant our babes into a bigger pot, planting by the moon helps us approach our plant care regimen with intention and purpose. It isn't always possible or feasible to do so, but I find working as closely as I can to it to be a magically rewarding endeavor.

Green Gnosis

PART FOUR

After reading this chapter, take a few moments to reflect on your plants and your plant care needs. In your journal create a weekly schedule for plant care including watering, trimming, checking for pests, and preventative care.

Chapter Five

Living Altars

Plants do not speak, but their
silence is alive with change.

. . .

May Sarton, *Plant Dreaming Deep*

Now that we have talked about the energy, spirits, and essence of the green flame and you have a basic intuitive understanding of what we are tapping into when we work with it, it is time to talk a little bit more about the everyday practices and workings that will help make your plant care something extraordinary and undeniably magical.

An altar is a space that we have deemed sacred; it is where we meet the spirit world halfway and perform acts of magic and devotion. They are great to have, like direct lines to the energies and spirits that we hold most dear. As a lifelong occultist who is partnered to other occultists, my home is full of altars, and I wouldn't have it any other way. When I first began a formal study in houseplant magic, naturally my immediate urge was to build another altar and fill it with statues of green gods. However, I soon realized that in doing so I was missing the point.

Most witches have a main altar where they perform the bulk of their work. As I began working with houseplants and understanding their unique traits, I started to include them on my main altar. Eventually all the other altars around the house got their own houseplants, too. Then it dawned on me: the green flame is pervasive, and it is going to do exactly what plants do when they are comfortable: grow! This was a game changer, and I started to look at each pot as a potential altar or working. Instead of trying to contain the green flame in one sacred space, I figured why not let it branch out into my entire home and help make it a sacred space.

Now, truthfully, I have what legally might be considered an obscene amount of houseplants, so the task of filling my home with the energy of the green flame in this way was not a difficult one. But even if you only have one houseplant sitting on a shelf somewhere, it will grow and spread its energy outward into your home; also, chances are you will have more soon because houseplants are addictive and easy to propagate. Knowing this and even planning for it can afford you some interesting opportunities in magic that you might otherwise miss out on.

Instead of building an altar to the green flame itself or to the green spirits, work with your planters as altars and your plants as the living embodiments of the energies you venerate—way cooler than a statue, right? Every plant emanates the energy of the green flame, and every planter becomes an amplifier for that energy. Working with them in this way allows us to use the energy of the green flame as a supportive energy throughout the home. Let's look at a few ways this can be done.

The Devotional Planter

These are planters where you raise a plant or multiple plants in honor of a deity or spirit. This can be designated to the plant spirit of the specific plant you are growing or to someone else. The plant spirit will always be present to some extent; however, if you aren't working with it directly, it is perfectly fine sharing that specimen.

Planters or containers should be marked with symbols of the spirit being honored, have plants that are related to them (if only by your own association), and be planted intentionally for the purpose of honoring this spirit. You don't want to just take a pot you already have with plants in it and declare it the "sacred pot of so-and-so." Instead, carefully consider every aspect of its construction and have an intention for each piece.

On the outside you can paint or embellish it, if you like, or you can choose a design that reminds you of them in some way. Inside the pot bury an image, be it a small statue or photo, of this spirit and include a handful of small nontoxic items that you might also associate with them.

When you plant something in it, make sure that the roots will be able to freely move and won't be restricted by what you are placing in the pot. You should avoid anything sharp as well, as I can tell you from personal experience that it is easy to forget there is a pokey thing to worry about. Otherwise, avoid anything that might leach plastics or other toxins into the soil—basically anything that might harm the plant.

Place these near your devotional altars or in spaces where you want to anchor this energy. It is also a really great way to be sneaky with your deity altars by hiding them in plain sight.

Must-Have Devotional Containers

In addition to a basic devotional container that can be made for a specific deity, there are two starter devotional containers that I recommend witches construct for their practice, the "self container" (I know—creative, right?) and the green guide container. Both have a special place in the home and a special job in our magical lives.

The Self Container

This is a devotional container made to develop a relationship with yourself. While it may sound a little strange, the concept is rooted in solid magical theory. Life is hard. You probably don't have a cheerleader to help encourage you through the difficult times, and like most magical people, you probably are the one being a cheerleader for other people in your life. This container is meant for you to be a living space where you devote time, attention, and energy to your own hopes and dreams. For those of us who feel guilty about taking time out of a busy schedule or taking attention away from those we care for, this can also be a way for us to carve out a little space and time for ourselves. Put it somewhere you will see it daily so that even if you aren't spending time directly with it, it remains part of your surroundings. As it grows, let it be a reminder that you are growing, too.

For this you will want to work with a plant or plants that you know are most likely to survive, like those listed in chapter 1. You will also need three personal items that represent you. As gross as it sounds, I recommend toenail clippings (to keep you grounded), discarded hair (to keep you anchored in the spiritual), and a sigil representing you, like the one that we made in chapter 3.

The Green Guide Container

This is a container made to act as a meeting place for you and your green guide(s). Again, I recommend using easy-to-care-for plants, but if you already have a plant associated with your green guides, then by all means, go for it! For this you will need three pieces of clear quartz that have been cleansed and then charged under the sun (*Crystal Magic for the Modern Witch* goes into detail about how to do this; you can also find handy tutorials online). Place the crystals in your substrate and then recite the following incantation before planting it with your chosen allies.

> Guiding spirits of the green flame
> I call out and summon you by name!
> Imbue this pot with your essence
> Make it brim with quintessence.
> Let this be our sacred space
> A beacon of your light and grace.

Frequency Planter

These are planters consisting of plants you are growing to bring specific energetic properties into your home. The plant spirit is respected but not honored in a regular devotional way here. The main point of this planter is to essentially act as a transmitter for a corresponding energy associated with that plant. For example, a frequency planter made to bring peace into the home might have a peace lily and some tradescantia growing inside it. One made to bring the energies of success into the office might be growing Chinese money plant (*Pilea peperomioides*) or perhaps string of pearls (*Senecio rowleyanus*).

The planter should be of a corresponding color, and inside should go crystals that also correspond with the same energy. These are meant to be passive systems that act like fountains for energy in your home.

Spell Planter

Spell planters are like frequency planters in that their job is to be a fountain for energy in your home, but instead of these being passive systems devoted to one form of energy, they are active systems devoted to multiple forms of energy. Treat the container as if it were a cauldron and everything inside of it an ingredient, including the plants. Think of the plant growth above the soil or substrate as the physical representation of the spell manifesting in real time. You will need to keep an eye on this container as its success or failure should be interpreted as part of the spell. Yes, that means if the plants fail, then your spell likely did, too. But it also means that if you keep the plants alive, you keep the magic alive as well.

My favorite part about working magic in this way is that it is so easy to cheat! Spell containers can be filled with easy-to-care-for plants, fed fertilizers and supplements, given their own lamp, and coaxed into being successful. You can work with them in real time to ensure that everything is being done to keep your magic from failing in a way that you just can't do with other types of magic. The only caveat is that the magic is slower than other forms of magic. A candle spell is going to be much faster at producing results than a living plant spell. So we have to think strategically and offensively.

Spells for instant cash aren't exactly going to work well in a spell container, but magic for long-term financial growth and stability would. Similarly, a spell for immediate healing for someone who just had a stroke wouldn't be ideal for something like this, but a spell to help keep people healthy or for long-term healing would.

Also, while the plants are technically ingredients in the metaphorical cauldron, they are also living things, and the point is to keep them alive and work with that living vitality. This isn't going to be the type of spell that you do and then forget about or do and then throw out the remains. Instead, this is going to be a working that you invest in over time and that has a partner, the plant spirit, who can just as easily make the working less effective as they can more effective based on how you treat them. To that end, be sure to make offerings to the plant spirit when the working is successful. In my practices, I find that the plant spirits I partner with enjoy offerings of crystals, blessed soil amendments, and adoration.

Must-Have Spell Planters

You will undoubtedly find a million ways to work with spell containers, and we will discuss various techniques throughout the rest of the book where they will come in handy. For now, I'd like to share two of the most important spell containers I have and how to construct them for yourself.

Sanctuary Spell Container

Your home should be a sanctuary! You should feel safe and comfortable in your environment, and it should nourish your mind, body, and soul. I created this spell container to transmute negative energy and keep the peace. I gathered all my supplies first and then cleansed and empowered each one before constructing the entire container. Doing it this way will allow you to add each item as you mention them in the incantation.

For this you will need a plant that is a known air purifier such as spider plant (*Chlorophytum comosum*), broad leaf palm (*Rhapis excelsa*), weeping fig (*Ficus benjamina*), peace lily (*Spathiphyllum*), Chinese evergreen (*Aglaonema*), or devil's ivy (*Epipremnum aurea)*. As part of your preparation, reach out to the plant spirit and let it know your intention with including it in this spell and what you expect it to do.

You will also need a black container, substrate, three pieces of charcoal, a white four-by-four-inch piece of paper, and something to write with. On the paper draw the sigil for peace and sanctuary shown below or create your own using the method in chapter 3. Creating your own sigil is a great opportunity to personalize a working. For example, you could create one using the word *sanctuary* as well as the names of the individuals living in your home or you could incorporate your address into it.

SIGIL FOR PEACE AND SANCTUARY

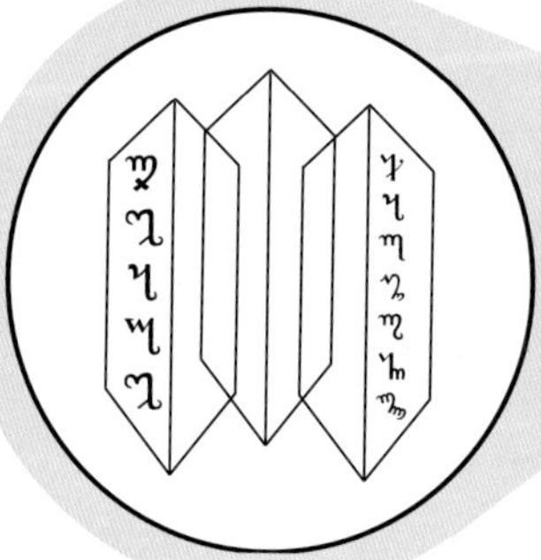

Fold this paper three times, each time folding the paper toward you and then rotating it clockwise before making the next fold. Charcoal is a natural purifier and a common additive to substrates whose job in this spell is to help purify energy moving through your space. Once you have everything collected, add the ingredients one by one as you put them in the container, saying:

> Black pot, black pot, full of peaceful magic
> Black pot, black pot, repelling all things tragic.
> In you I place these items of power
> One by one to keep things from going sour.
> First the soil to lay the ground
> A substrate for magic profound.
> Then the charcoal to clear the air
> To sooth tempers and calm the scare.
> Next a sigil of power for command
> Directing this working to be grand.
> Last not least my verdant ally
> A plant I grow who all abide by.

Black pot, black pot, full of peaceful magic
Black pot, black pot, repelling all things tragic.
With you I cast this verdant spell
To be a sanctuary from what feels like hell.

Once you are finished, use more soil to fill in the remaining space. Place in a location where you will see it and where others will as well. This is excellent in living, dining, or bedrooms.

Protection Spell Container

Protection is something we all need. We need to be protected from accidents, each other, and even nature itself. When working forms of protection magic with the plant kingdom, traditionally we choose plants with spines, needles, and generally anything that can make touching it an uncomfortable experience. Cactuses are excellent for this form of protection and are super easy to grow. If you can get away with growing a cactus in your home, then I highly recommend it.

Some folks, however, worry about growing something like a cactus in their home; after all, they do cause pain when you touch them. For years, my partner was against raising cactuses inside our home. He didn't like that every time you need to move anywhere near their vicinity, you have to be on guard or you might accidently touch a needle. Living in the western United States, however, means that we have regular access to some truly stunning and rare cactuses. Whenever I would go plant shopping, I would inevitably find a cactus that was just weird enough to fit in with my collection and bring it home. Two or three days later, I'd find that the cactus had been moved either to my office or the patio. No cactuses allowed!

FIVE SAFER CACTI

That is, until we found the right kind of cactus to work with inside our home; it turns out not all of them are spiky death clubs! If you are interested in raising a cactus for protection magic and want minimal personal risk due to those powerful needles, you might want to check out these safer cacti. It should be noted, however, that needles are part of what makes a cactus a cactus. In fact, it is the defining feature that sets them apart from other succulents. So while these cactuses are easier to handle and live with in the home, they are still pointy little shits that should be respected at all costs. For a list of non-pokey protection plants, check out the end of this working.

AFRICAN MILK TREE (*Euphorbia trigona*) is a fun cactus that can grow up to six feet in the wild, but in your home you can expect it to reach up to five feet. Its needles are smaller and more compact, and it comes in an array of colors, from white to red.

BOOBIE CACTUS (*Myrtillocactus geometrizans* 'Fukurokuryuzinboku') is shaped like a tower of breasts and has small needles at the tips of each leaf. This is especially good for protection against sexual assault and is deeply connected to the divine female.

PINCUSHION CACTUS (*Euphorbia obesa*) grows in a geometrical round shape, is a slow grower, and has small needles along its spines that are avoidable.

MEXICAN FENCE POST CACTUS (*Pachycereus marginatus*) is a columnar cactus that grows upright without branching and has five to seven spines. The flesh is dark green, its ridges are white, and short needles mature to black.

HOLIDAY CACTUS (*Schlumbergera*) is a trailing cactus that produces vibrant flowers in the fall and winter. The spines of this cactus are short and easily avoided.

Back to Our Working...

Once you have found the right plant to partner with for your protection spell container, the working itself is simple. In addition to the plant, you will need five river rocks or palm stones, a small piece of paper, something to write with, a metallic permanent marker or paint and brush to put symbols on those stones, a black container, and substrate.

Somewhere on the container, draw or paint the sigil for the green flame that you created in chapter 3. Around that symbol draw or paint the shape of a shield. Using my sigil from the earlier example, the drawing looks like this. It can be placed anywhere on the container, inside or out, and is a modified sigil for working with the protective forces of the green flame.

« GREEN FLAME AND SHIELD SIGIL

On each of the stones draw or paint a pentacle. Next, on a small piece of paper, draw the sigil for your green name (or if you are casting this spell on behalf of someone else, a sigil representing their name). Additionally, you can create a sigil representing an address when working on a whole residence. Set everything aside until it has dried.

Gather the rest of your ingredients. When you are ready, recite the following incantation as you assemble the spell. Place a little bit of dirt in the container to start, and then add each ingredient as you say its name in the incantation.

Once you are finished, use more soil to fill in the remaining space and place the container near your altar or, if possible, your front door.

> By the green flame I cast this spell
> Let the heavens quake and power swell!
> Into this pot I place three stones
> To protect and serve and be its bones.
> Now I place this sacred sigil
> A symbol that marks whom to vigil.
> Last I plant my beloved friend
> And trust that they will be with me until the end.
> Let no harm come or calamity stay
> Be a sentinel and keep evil at bay.
> This is my will and so it shall be
> For the good of all but mostly for me!

FIVE NON-POKEY PROTECTION PLANTS

The protective qualities of these plants come from their propensity to grow in ways that conceal or camouflage. If cactuses aren't going to work in your living space or you are interested in something a little different, check out these plants.

ELEPHANT EARS (*Alocasia*, *Colocasia*, and *Caladium*) grow large, broad leaves in a myriad of colors and shapes that are excellent at helping hide and camouflage.

MONSTERAS (entire genus) have large leaves and thick vines that are excellent at concealing and hiding things. Their name means "monstrous" because of the large masked look of their leaves, which also makes them great at projecting the illusion that something big and scary is protecting you.

PHILODENDRONS (entire genus) are fantastic at projecting energy outward, and their big leaves can resemble shields.

BAMBOOS (entire genus) are fast-growing plants that require a lot of light but whose strong timber-like stalks make an effective energy barrier. Not to be confused with lucky bamboo, which is actually a species of *Dracaena*.

SNAKE PLANTS (*Sansevieria*) have large thin leaves that are durable and cut through anything in their way. They make excellent protection partners, especially near the front door of the home.

Divination Container

The next type of houseplant container working are those that are made for the purposes of divination. I have grown quite fond of these over the years and find that if you are someone who enjoys scrying and gazing, then this will all come naturally to you. The plants we choose to work with in this container will be those who have variegation that is not static, meaning that each leaf has a different variegation pattern. This is important because as part of this working we will be asking the plant a question and then discerning the answer based on how the next leaf unfolds and what it looks like.

The idea here is to have a conversation with the plant spirit, one that allows us to seek direct answers or have a bit of back and forth if needed. For this to work successfully, not only should the plant be variegated, but it also should be a relatively fast grower. Working with slower-growing plants is fine, but it can feel a bit like waiting on a letter to be delivered by horseback from the opposite side of the continent.

Before we go into how to build this working container or what to look for on the leaves, let's take a moment to discuss five top performing plants that provide excellent foliage to divine messages from.

FIVE LEAVES WORTH SCRYING OVER

Here are a few of my preferred plants to work with in divination containers. Again, all of these are variegated plants.

COLOCASIA ESCULENTA 'Mojito' is at the top of my list because it produces large leaves with a lot of surface area to view. Its variegation is also in a constellation pattern, meaning that it mostly spreads outward in flecks from the stem, resembling the night sky. You can expect a new leaf once every week during peak growing season.

EPIPREMNUM AUREUM Also known as pothos or devil's ivy, this has a golden variegation that usually appears in lines and streaks. You can expect one or two new leaves a week during peak growing season. *Epipremnum aureum* 'Glacier' (also known as glacier pothos) is a variety that has large chunky white variegation, as do the cultivars 'Pearls of Jade' and 'Pothos N-Joy'. The cultivars 'Manjula' and 'Marble Queen' have splashy white and green variegation and make fantastic patterns. Lastly, the cultivars 'Global Green' and 'Jessenia' have green and light green to yellow variegation that typically spread across the leaf.

EPIPREMNUM PINNATUM 'Albo variegata' is a fast-growing sister to *E. aureum*, which doesn't have nearly as many cultivars on the market but does have fascinating splashy white variegation that is excellent for scrying. The leaves of this species also size up well when given a pole. You can expect a new leaf once every week to two weeks during peak growing season.

MONSTERA DELICIOSA 'Albo variegata' is a large-leafed cultivar that is great for scrying. It is a moderate grower with new leaves expected every two weeks during peak season. You can also find a much pricier golden variegation of this species called the *Monstera Aurea*. Similarly, there is the *Monstera deliciosa* 'Thai constellation' that has golden variegation presented in a constellation pattern.

SYNGONIUM PODOPHYLLUM VARIEGATA or any variegated cultivar of *S. podophyllum* will make an excellent companion in scrying and divination work. I particularly recommend 'Albo', 'Aurea', and 'Mojito' for this purpose.

Building the Container

For this working, I like to keep it simple. You will need a blue, purple, black, white, or gray container, seven pieces of clear quartz, a piece of paper and something to write with, the plant you will be working with, and your substrate of choice.

Before you start the working, cleanse the container using your preferred cleansing method. If you aren't familiar with cleansing, passing the pot through some myrrh or frankincense incense will work wonderfully. You will need to cleanse and charge the crystals under the full moon. To do this, take them outside and allow them to bathe in moonlight for a few hours; when finished, program them by sending the mental intention for them to aid the plant to bring clear and meaningful messages through its leaves.

On a piece of paper, draw an eyeball with an empty circle where the pupil should be. Inside of that space, draw the sigil you created for the green flame at the end of chapter 3. This is a modified green flame sigil for divination. Using my sigil example from before, this is what that modified figure should look like.

GREEN FLAME DIVINATION SIGIL

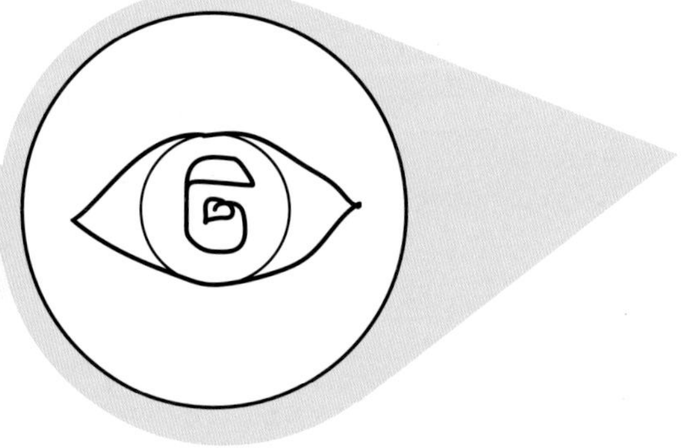

Pot up your container, including the substrate, crystals, sigil paper, and plant. Make sure to spread the crystals out the best you can and shake the pot just a bit to let substrate enter spaces between the crystals. When you have repotted the plant and all the pieces of the working are inside the container, place one hand on either side of the pot and recite the following incantation.

> Ally from the green flame, a verdant mystery now revealed.
> I conjure thee, O emerald eye, to make seen what has been sealed.
> Part the worlds and quake the earth, I place this task on you.
> Upon each leaf a message to divine something useful and true!
> Speak through color and speak through form and vein,
> For with this spell I summon fast an ally who can't be slain.

Varieomancy

Varieomancy is the art of divining omens through studying the colors and patterns made by variegation on the newly emerged leaf of a living plant. Haven't heard of it? That is because I discovered it and this is the first time, to the best of my knowledge, that it is being written about in print. I have been doing it for years and assumed it was a thing that other people did; however, when I went looking for what it was called, I learned that no such practice is listed anywhere. The closest I could find was tasseomancy, also known as tea leaf reading, so I gave it a name, and here we are!

It isn't very complicated, and while you do not need a divination container as discussed in the last section, they will make this whole practice a lot easier. Here is my three-step guide to varieomancy.

STEP ONE: Partner with a plant specifically for this type of divination. Ask the plant spirit to reveal the answer to a question you have, and then ask the plant. Request that it respond by expressing discernable patterns that will convey its answer in the next leaf to emerge. You can also simply ask for the leaf to reveal a message about the coming week after it has unfolded.

STEP TWO: Wait for the leaf to emerge and for it to harden off. New leaves need a day or two, sometimes more, to fully take shape and express all the colors they are capable of. Wait for the leaf to deepen in color and to completely express all patterns.

STEP THREE: Once the leaf has hardened off, take a look at the variegation displayed and look for symbols, directional patterns, and how color is expressed throughout the leaf. Over time you will develop your own language with the patterns expressed, but for now I recommend using the classic symbols associated with tea leaf reading. They are used in other systems of divination, such as Lenormand cards, and are already associated with tea leaf reading, so it's not a stretch by any means. Here is a chart of symbols and their meanings, inspired by the traditional symbols used in tasseomancy.

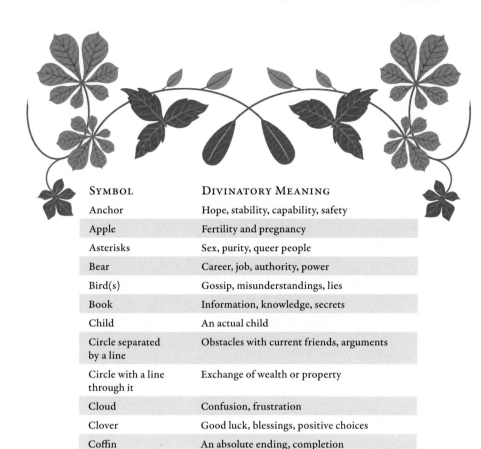

Symbol	Divinatory Meaning
Anchor	Hope, stability, capability, safety
Apple	Fertility and pregnancy
Asterisks	Sex, purity, queer people
Bear	Career, job, authority, power
Bird(s)	Gossip, misunderstandings, lies
Book	Information, knowledge, secrets
Child	An actual child
Circle separated by a line	Obstacles with current friends, arguments
Circle with a line through it	Exchange of wealth or property
Cloud	Confusion, frustration
Clover	Good luck, blessings, positive choices
Coffin	An absolute ending, completion
Cross	Burden, weight, stress
Diamond	Loyalty and trust
Dog	True friendship, plutonic love
Fish	Prosperous work and finances
Flower	New happiness or reason to celebrate, joy
Fox	Need to move forward carefully, move with cunning
Garden	Social engagements, community, party
Gun	Fighting, setbacks, battle
Hammer	Hard work and physical labor
Hand	Physical body and health
Heart	True love, hot romance, spiritual connection
House/doorway	Security, safety, sanctuary

Symbol	Divinatory Meaning
Key	Opportunity, changing circumstances
Letter	Important news, email, message
Mice	Missing information, lies
Moon	High emotions, suspicion
Mountain	Obstacles and challenges
Path/crossroad	Important decisions, fork in road
Phallus	New romance, sex
Purse	Accounts, wallet, purse
Rider	New beginning, inspiration
Ring	Connection, partnership, marriage
Scythe	Harvest, clearing a path, separation
Shield	Fear mongering, enemies, do not trust
Ship	Movement, journey, adventure
Smile	Happiness, wishes granted
Snake	Someone close is up to no good
Square	Unexpected gifts
Star	Hope, looking ahead, planning
Stork	Big news, pregnancy, new things coming
Sun	Success, wealth, positive outcome
The number 7	Luck and chance
Tower	Need for awareness, distraction, temptations
Tree	Traditions, lineage, values
Two circles separated by two lines	Separation, arguments, polarization
Two intersecting circles	New allies or friendships
Whip	Punishment, discipline, unrest
XX	Illness, disease, possible death

The rest is up to your intuition. Because variegation is mutable, the leaf will look different from the others on the plant. Compare them. Does your new leaf have more or less variegation than the others? How do you interpret that? For me, that depends on the question I asked and the plant I was working with. In general, I would say more variegation is a positive thing and less would be bad.

If the leaf is more colorful than others, I would take that as a positive sign as well. The same would be said for instances where the leaf was expressing a desired amount of variegation.

If the leaf is malformed or if it develops partially, then drops, or if the variegation totally covers the leaves and makes that leaf incapable of producing photosynthesis (which can happen with 'Albo' and 'Aurea' variegated plants), then I would interpret all of those as bad omens—most likely blockages and false starts.

Work with the symbols you see in the leaf. Try gazing into it and letting your mind wander; see what thoughts and images surface. Listen to your intuition. If you come across something that doesn't make sense, ask your guides for clarity. Like any form of scrying and divination, you have to trust yourself and see where the reading takes you!

CHAPTER FIVE

Green Gnosis

PART FIVE

After reading this chapter's text and reflecting on your own magical practice and needs, respond to the following prompts in your journal.

- *Have you put a living plant on your personal working altar in the past? If so, which plant(s) and why?*
- *Who is a deity you would consider creating a devotional planter for? What plant(s) would you choose to put in it and why?*
- *Taking a moment to reflect on your home environment, what are energies that you would like to bring into it? What energies would you like to see changed? What plants could you include in a frequency or spell container to help attract those energies?*
- *Taking a moment to reflect on your daily life and routine, what are questions that you could ask a plant that would make your life smoother and easier? What blocks do you normally encounter?*

Chapter Six

Sacred Substrates

A plant needs to do more than stretch its leaves toward the sun. It also needs to send down roots deep into the ground. They hold on tightly in the dark, out of sight where it is easy to forget about them. But it is the fact that a plant can do these two things at once, anchoring itself to the earth even as it reaches for the sky, that makes it strong.

. . .

Cameron Dokey, *Kissed*

Had you told me as a young man that I would one day be writing about dirt as an adult, I might have made different life choices. But here we are, and believe it or not, there is a whole bunch to discuss on the matter. You see, what we plant our green friends in is just as important as the plants themselves. Substrates are at least half of the equation; when prepared correctly for the plant's needs, they not only help ensure that your plant can survive, but they also can be the first line of defense when keeping them safe from pests and potential rot. Even more so, the components that comprise our substrates can give us a whole new layer of magic to work with our indoor plants. In this chapter we are going to explore the mundane and spiritual components of soils and substrates and jump into how we can work with them to enhance the magic performed with our plants.

To be technical, a substrate—most often soil—is the medium in which we grow our houseplants. This is usually a soil mix of some sort, but it can also be fir bark, coco coir, LECA (an acronym for lightweight expanded clay aggregate), and even straw! In general, soil is a substrate that is made up of various small particles of decaying biological matter and other aggregates like sand, perlites, etc. Not all substrates are soils; some substrates are soilless and consist of large aggregates and no small particles.

One of the biggest parts of our job is to ensure that each of the plants we care for has the right kind of substrate to grow in. Choosing the wrong type of substrate is one of the largest contributing factors to a plant's death indoors, and not all substrates are cut out for giving our plants what they need. A key factor with this is that the substrates plants come in from big box stores and nurseries are mixed to work with the growers' conditions, not necessarily the conditions of your home. For the most part, by the time a plant makes it to your home, it is not only ready to be repotted, but it will also need substrate that is right for your conditions.

Let's take a look at the most common forms of substrate and substrate aggregates and what they are used for.

Aggregates

Aggregates are soil particle components that bind together. The space between aggregates provides pores that assist in the movement of water and air within the soil as well as root growth. Denser soils are made up of smaller aggregates that bind together and fill in pores, reducing the movement of oxygen and water and making it more difficult for larger roots to form. Denser aggregates are easily moved by outside forces (like when water is applied and settles into existing crevices), sealing off pores and airflow. Each aggregate has an elemental correspondence that connects them to the primary forces governing the universe as well as gives us access to them. Each substrate is its own mix of these forces; knowing what they are and how they affect the energy of our plants is invaluable to us as hortocculturists.

Chunkier/looser soils have the opposite problem—they have a harder time retaining moisture and provide an excess of air to the roots. The balance between these two extremes is referred to as aggregate stability. Jot that down; it will be on the test! (Not really.)

When you are creating the right substrate for your plant, you have to consider what type of aggregate balance it is going to require. We then work with the following ingredients to build the best substrate for our plant and its required conditions.

COCO COIR is ultra-fine ground coconut husk that makes an excellent substrate for seeds and seedlings and is often used as the base for many soil recipes. It absorbs water easily; however, it also dries out easily on its own and has very little nutritional value for plants. It corresponds with the element of air.

COCO HUSK, also corresponding with the element of air, is coconut bark. It is usually sold in large chunks and used primarily by those who raise epiphytic plants (such as orchids, anthuriums, and hoya) because it absorbs just enough water without saturating the roots of these plants. This is often sold as bedding for reptile habitats in addition to being marketed to gardeners. Beware, however: the coco husk available through pet retailers has often been cleaned in ocean water, which is absorbed into the husk and can be released when reintroduced to water. This means that you may end up with tiny salt crystals forming around your roots that can kill the plant. If you purchase coco husk from a pet retailer, be sure to soak it overnight and give it a good rinse to release any unwanted salts before using it. Coco husk sold specifically for plants has usually been cleaned with freshwater.

FIR BARK corresponds with the element of earth and is used mostly by those who grow epiphytic plants, as it is great at absorbing just enough water to keep roots humid and moist without oversaturating them. It provides minimal nutrition to the plants and smells amazing. I do not use it as a solo act, but it is a favorite to add to chunkier soils. Keep in mind this is not fir mulch, which can also be used but is more likely to contain pests and finer pieces.

HORTICULTURAL CHARCOAL is chemical-free natural hardwood that has been charred and corresponds with the element of fire. It is used in substrates to provide aeration and help keep mold and fungus from developing. Activated charcoal is similar; however, it has been powdered and reconstituted into the shape of (most often) tiny pellets. It is prized for its added ability to absorb smells and toxins because this process creates tiny holes that act as filters. Activated charcoal is used in aquarium filters for this purpose and can be added to hydroponic/semi-hydroponic setups to provide the same benefit. It is always recommended to use charcoals in terrarium setups, especially the activated variety. Both release carbon into substrates that is readily used by all plants.

LECA (lightweight expanded clay aggregate) is expanded clay pebbles that are prized by those who prefer hydroponic/semi-hydroponic setups. Corresponding with the element of air, it does an excellent job at retaining both oxygen and water, and it is known to wick water up from shallow wells that pool in the bottom of containers. It can be added to soil mixes to loosen and provide aeration or be used alone. It provides no nutritional value to the plants, however. Like perlite and vermiculite, LECA can also be used in propagation.

LOAM corresponds with the element of earth and usually consists of roughly 40 percent sand, 40 percent silt, and 20 percent clay and makes for a fine but fertile substrate. Because it is so fine, it makes for a dense and even paste-like consistency when wet, so it should be amended with perlite or other larger aggregates. Alone, it can clog roots. Often you will see the term "loamy" used to describe soil type; this generally means that it should have lots of fine particles and be on the denser side.

PEAT MOSS corresponds with the element of earth and is the decayed remains of plants (and sometimes animals) that is dug up from wetlands and used as a base in a lot of substrate mixes. It can absorb twenty times its weight in water and is very fine and loaded with nutrients. The problem with peat moss is that it (and the next moss we are going to talk about) are being overharvested. It also can't be reused or separated out after it has been added, so it is a one-time thing. With a pH of 3.5–4.0, peat is also highly acidic.

PERLITE is expanded volcanic glass that usually comes in small white chunks that are found in soil mixes. It corresponds with the element of fire and is used primarily to provide aeration to soil; however, it can be used as a semi-hydroponic medium, similar to LECA. It has no nutritional value to the plants; however, it does help absorb excess water. Add perlite to dense substrates/mixes to provide oxygen to roots and to help break up clumpy soil. Perlite is also an excellent aid when propagating plants from cuttings. For more on this, see the propagation section in chapter 4.

PUMICE is similar to perlite in every way that counts: it is a type of volcanic glass used to bring aeration to denser soils and help retain water in sandier soils. Corresponding with the element of fire, it is also typically two to three times the cost of perlite. I typically add this to succulent mixes, some of my semi-hydro substrate blends, and as a decorative substrate topping for cactuses. Pumice doesn't break down as easily as perlite, and it is reusable in a way that perlite tends not to be.

SAND needs no explanation. Corresponding with the element of water, it actually has a lot of potential uses as a substrate or in a substrate mix because it evenly absorbs water. Because it is so fine, sand can be used to help anchor roots or create a denser substrate mix. As a solo act, sand is only a good substrate for a handful of plants, but when added to other substrates or when treated with nutrients, it can be a versatile ingredient that strengthens soil. I prefer to use the cheap pool filter sand as it is more on the dust-free side, has been cleaned and sterilized, and has a consistent grain. Sand is mostly silica, which both enhances psychic ability and retains a psychic charge for long periods of time. In containers this will help stabilize the energy of the magic you are doing and boost the production of that magic.

SPHAGNUM MOSS is a mostly self-sustaining form of long strand moss that is harvested from tropical climates like New Zealand and part of Asia and corresponds with the element of water. In some regions it is considered to be overharvested; however, there are many farms that grow renewably. Once it dies back, it easily absorbs water and also contains special properties that naturally preserve it against decomposition. Many varieties of sphagnum also contain natural antifungal properties. It is most often used to aid in propagation and can be added to substrates to assist in moisture retention. While many of us love to use this moss because it is so versatile, it is a resource that we are running out of on the planet. Many people do not know that it can be reused or that most often you can revive the dried moss and grow it yourself! While I caution its overuse, I do recommend procuring some and reviving it so you can grow your plants in living moss (which is super cool) or that you find a grower online who is selling live sphagnum moss. It is very easy to take care of and can be a living substrate for you to grow your plants in. I will discuss this more when we get to mosses later in the book.

VERMICULITE is expanded biolite, which is a mineral formed of various biological components that greatly increases in size when heated. It corresponds with the element of earth. Highly absorbent, it is used as a substrate and added to substrates because of its capacity to retain water. It has no nutritional value to the plants; however, it is highly prized for its ability to release water in line with the plant's needs. Vermiculite can be added to drier mixes to provide moisture retention and is often used to assist in propagation.

pH Levels

pH is a measure of the acidity or alkalinity of water and solutions. In horticulture, we measure the pH of the water we are using to hydrate our plants as well as the substrate itself. As you have seen, the ingredients we use to create a substrate can affect the overall pH of the mix. Why we care about this is because pH levels can drastically impact a plant's ability to absorb nutrients and water. Low pH can make a plant develop calcium and magnesium deficiencies; on the other hand, a high pH can cause a plant to develop iron deficiencies and chlorosis (a yellowing of the leaves that is caused by low chlorophyl production).

The pH scale runs from 0 to 14, with acidity levels decreasing and alkalinity increasing as the numbers rise, with 7 being considered neutral. Most houseplants enjoy pH levels between 6 and 7, where vital micronutrients like calcium, sulphur, potassium, and others are made more readily available for the plant. Some plants, like carnivorous plants, African violets, and ferns, enjoy acidic soil that reaches in some instances as low as 3.5 in pH levels. Others, like aloes, enjoy increased alkaline in their substrates that can get as high as 8.5. Always be sure to do a little research about what your plant likes. Each of those listed in the index enjoy a basic soil pH between 6 and 7 unless otherwise noted.

Most all-purpose soils are within the neutral range and require little additives. If you are making your own, like I prefer to do, then you will want to test the pH levels of your substrate before you begin planting. You also might want to check the pH levels of substrates used with underperforming plants as this is a common cause of problems. There are two elements to consider here: the pH levels of the water as well as the soil you are using. Again, in most instances an all-purpose mix should be neutral, and so the only thing to really worry about is the water you are using. I recommend testing them both. You can purchase a cheap and easy pH test system at most hardware and pet supply stores as well as online. Each of them will require something different, but the mechanics are all the same.

When testing water pH, you are going to collect a sample either by dunking a test strip into the water for a few seconds or dropping a chemical into a test tube to see what color the water changes. Again, follow the instructions.

When testing soil pH, you will actually be testing the runoff water. Either collect a sample from the bottom of the tray after watering or grab a handful of recently watered substrate and squeeze until enough water is collected to perform the test. Alternatively, you can buy an electronic testing device or automatic tester that you just stick in your substrate and it will give you a measurement.

Adjusting pH is more difficult in substrates than it is water, though neither is super fun. For water, you can buy a product called "pH Up" and another called "pH Down," most easily found in pet stores with aquarium supplies. Be careful, though, as once you start tinkering with pH levels, it can be difficult to bring things back to neutral once you have used the solutions to go too far in one direction. For organic options, you can try using a tea made from the soil additives in the next section.

Adjusting substrate pH takes more time, sometimes weeks, but is always worth it if your plants are struggling. This is most easily done by the addition of soil amendments.

Additives and Fertilizers

Substrates don't always come with everything a plant needs to thrive, so we turn to additives and fertilizers to provide the necessary nutrients for our plants. As a general rule, I think of additives as corresponding with the element of earth and fertilizers as corresponding with fire. Remember, each additive has the potential to adjust pH levels.

Additives

COMPOST is decayed biomatter (usually dead leaves and vegetable scraps) that is loaded with nutrients and usually added as an amendment to soil. It is not generally advised to grow plants directly in compost as it tends to be too rich in nutrients and can kill the plant—oh, and let's not forget the smell! Compost makes for a great natural fertilizer, however, and if you are lucky enough to make your own, you can have a lot of control over what does or doesn't make it into your mix. Compost tends to be acidic and usually requires a sweetening agent like lime to balance pH.

MANURE is used a lot in horticulture because it is the oldest natural fertilizer known to us. Like compost, it is loaded with nutrients and can burn out plants if used in great quantities. Generally, I avoid manure at all costs because most houseplants do not like heavy fertilizers and it stinks to high heaven. Even a little bit in your substrate can overpower the best scented candle, and it attracts pests! Feel free to use manure if you feel inclined—in small amounts houseplants can love it—but I tend to go with something a little lighter such as worm castings.

WORM CASTINGS are technically a type of manure; however, they don't smell and are much weaker in nutrition than, say, cow manure, so plants aren't going to get burnt out. Worm castings are fine and powdery so they will make soil denser when added.

LIME is powdered limestone, which is a sweetening agent added to substrates to reduce acidity. Not all limes are suitable for gardening, however, so make sure you procure gardening lime. Also, be sure to test your pH levels prior to adding lime on your own as it can be difficult to readjust if you use too much. Caution is advised whenever you are adjusting substrate pH levels.

GYPSUM is a sulfate mineral that is powdered and used similarly to lime. It reduces the erosion of phosphorus, making it more absorbable to the plant.

In addition to adding compost, COFFEE GROUNDS are an excellent soil additive when you want to increase the acidity of the soil. This can affect everything from the color of a plant's leaves and flowers to how strong a stalk grows. Usually raising the acidity of houseplant soil is not required unless the substrate is homemade and lacks acidic ingredients or if it is older and those nutrients have already been used up by the plant. As with lime, you should do a soil test before adding anything that might affect pH.

Fertilizers

Chances are that if you bought a premixed bag of soil, it already has plenty of fertilizer in it; however, that fertilizer will probably run out after a few months. While most plants love fertilizer, not all do, so be sure to do your research on the specific species and its needs.

All fertilizers come with a breakdown of three vital nutrients they provide: nitrogen, phosphorus, and potassium. Nitrogen (presented by the letter N) helps your plants green up and aids in the production of photosynthesis. It is generally thought to be beneficial for any part of the plant that is aboveground. Phosphorus (P) helps with root development and can assist in bigger blooms in plants that flower. Potassium (K) promotes the general well-being of a plant and assists in every function it undergoes.

If you are doing everything right with watering, temperature, humidity, and light but your plants aren't looking too healthy, you might consider adding fertilizer to your regimen. Some plants need more of one of those numbers than others, so again, be sure to do your research. However, in general, an all-purpose fertilizer will do the trick! There are three methods for how to apply fertilizer.

LIQUID FERTILIZER is a concentrated form of fertilizer that is added to water before application. The nutrients become immediately available to the plant this way.

SLOW-RELEASE FERTILIZER usually comes in pellet form and is added to soil, where it will release small amounts of fertilizer each watering over the course of several months.

FOLIAR SPRAY FERTILIZER is a liquid fertilizer that is added to water and then sprayed on the leaves of the plant, where it is absorbed. The nutrients are immediately available to the plant; however, you must select a fertilizer specifically designed to be dispensed in this way. Regular fertilizers can kill leaves if applied directly. In general, for this method, a very mild amount is applied daily or weekly.

There are plenty of man-made fertilizers out there. I have no wish to tell you what to do, rather how *I* do things, and when it comes to fertilizers, I have a love-hate relationship. Manmade fertilizers have been crucial for our species, but they have also created a lot of environmental issues in some parts of the world. Additionally, the largest provider of commercial fertilizer on the globe is Miracle-Gro, which was owned by the Monsanto corporation, which was responsible for several environmental wrongs and for creating cancer-causing pesticides. This is another topic I am going to recommend you do some research on independently before you buy!

The fertilizer I love to use and share with the world is called liquid fish emulsion, which is essentially liquified fish. Some brands have a stronger smell than others; however, it is all natural and the plants seem to really enjoy it. Just like manure, a little bit can go a long way, so use it sparingly.

All fertilizers can be a bad thing when not properly mixed or when mixed at too great a strength. A favorite trick of mine is to water my plants weekly with a mix that is half strength to whatever the bottle recommends. I find this keeps them from burning up due to overexposure and avoids unwanted smells that can be strong at full strength when using natural fertilizers. It also allows me to see how my plants respond in real time so adjusting is easy.

Creating Your Substrate

You do not need to make your own soil mix, especially if you are new to houseplants. An all-purpose soil mix from the garden center will have everything you need to get your feet wet. The added pressure of creating your own soil mix can be an unnecessary burden in the beginning, especially when someone has already done it for you! On the other hand, after a plant or two, you will probably want to make your own or learn to amend the store-bought mix so that it better suits your specific needs.

I live by the general rule of thumb that the daintier the leaf, the loamier the soil. Plants like herbs require finer soils because they tend to have finer roots. On the other hand, rough and tumble succulents like fast-drying, low-quality soil. Here I will give you both my all-purpose mix and a recipe for amending the store-bought stuff.

A common mistake, and one that I made for years before correcting, is that darker soil doesn't necessarily mean it is more fertile. What it really means is that the aggregates that compose the soil are dark. I also learned that many of the companies that sell soil tend to dye them dark, so they look fertile. Homemade substrates can be on the lighter side, so don't stress!

The following measurements are in parts so you can easily adjust the recipe to make the quantity you need. Each element is represented in this recipe. As you add the aggregates and additives, take a second to connect with those elements mentally one by one. Grab a handful of each ingredient and think to yourself, "This is connected to the element of _____ and will connect my magic to that force for as long as this substrate is being used. It has power. My substrate has power."

All-Purpose Houseplant Substrate Recipe

2 parts coco coir (or peat moss; if so, use 1 tablespoon lime or gypsum to every gallon of peat)
1 part worm castings, manure, or compost
1 part vermiculite
1 part sand
1 part perlite or pumice
1 part charcoal

Blend until mixed well. Add optional slow-release fertilizer, following the instructions on the package for measurements.

Easy Store-Bought Soil Amendment

Often the store-bought stuff is a little too fine for most of the plants you will be growing indoors, especially the aroids. To fix this, mix two parts soil mix with one part perlite and one part fir bark (for dryer soils) or vermiculite (for moister soils), depending on how much moisture you want it to hold. When growing anthurium and larger aroids like philodendron and monstera,

I recommend using a size 3 or 4 perlite, which is much chunkier and will add the perfect amount of aeration to normal store-bought potting mix.

Let's Keep It Magical

Now that I have gone over all the necessary information, let's talk about how we as witches and occultists should approach the whole topic of soil and substrate. From a very practical point of view, substrates are the base of operation for the plant. It grows into and out of the substrate, and therefore we would be wise to prepare it and treat it with the utmost intention and respect.

As I was hinting at earlier, most substrates contain ingredients like sand and volcanic glass, which are excellent at retaining psychic imprints and as a result make for useful allies in magic. That means your soil mix is a psychic battery waiting to be charged and the perfect substrate for magic! There is a lot of decaying matter in soil as well as it being the place where the roots grow, which connect it to the underworld and the world of faery—two places where spirits freely roam and work magic. Your substrate isn't just dirt you are sticking a plant in; it is a programmable interface capable of bridging planes of existence and carrying a long-term psychic charge.

Substrate Activation

Once you have mixed your substrate together, you can cleanse and prepare it for magic (or, as I like to say in my ultra-geeky way, activate the substrate). This is the easiest thing you can do, and if you perform no other act from this book, let it be this one! Ground and center yourself in whatever way you are most comfortable, and then hold the bowl, tub, or bag of mix with both hands. Close your eyes and focus on the substrate. Take a moment to consider exactly what is in the mix and what it is there to do. Then, as if tipping your mind like a watering can, pour your consciousness into the substrate.

Imagine for a few moments that the substrate has absorbed your consciousness as though it were water and as it soaks you up, it also soaks in your instructions. If you have a specific working, like a love spell, go ahead and imprint that psychic energy by visualizing yourself happy with a partner or partners, and allow the substrate to absorb that image. For our purposes here, let's visualize the plant we intend to grow becoming strong and healthy. See it as a full-grown plant, full of verdancy and life, and allow that image to be absorbed into the substrate. See your psychic imprint overriding all other imprints until the substrate radiates that image back to you in your mind's eye and begins to glow green with the energy of the green flame.

Once you intuitively feel that the substrate has taken on as much psychic information as possible, stop sending it psychic energy and instead see any excess energy draining from the substrate like excess water, flowing down to the base of your feet, where it is collected by your own energy body and recycled.

Finish this working by opening your eyes, taking a deep breath, and then gently exhaling over the substrate before saying the following incantation.

> Behold the stars within the earth
> For from this soil magic shall birth!
> From its depths my ritual will reach
> Breaking free with lessons to teach.
> Retaining all of my psychic vision
> A secret place of my decision.
> With my mind I set the scene
> A substrate that burns a flame of green!

Magical Amendments

I tend to bury a lot of stuff in my flowerpots, especially once a working gets started and I want to adjust it or get more specific. A good example would be burying rose quartz in the substrate of a plant I am growing as part of a love spell to increase the working's self-respect or emotional healing elements. I have been known to add enchanted herbal mixes to the substrate to add a little extra oomph! If you think of your pots more like cauldrons and your substrate more like a potion, the potential for magic is really quite endless. Let's take a look at some abnormal aggregates that you might choose to include in your substrate.

CRYSTALS have already been part of the magic we discussed in the previous chapter. We work with them in hortocculture because they are themselves psychic generators of energy that are, for the most part, easy to clean and safe to bury. Not all crystals and minerals are suitable for this; some will deteriorate, and some are toxic to plant life. Avoid raw crystals such as selenite, which have small cracks that can erode over time, and crystals such as malachite that contain copper, which can harm root growth and leaf production.

HAIR AND NAIL CLIPPINGS are used in many workings when you want to connect the spell or ritual directly to a person without any energetic interference. While it might sound gross—and I am personally not into putting chunks of hair in my substrates—there is evidence to suggest that this can be beneficial to the plants. Some fertilizers even contain human hair.

PETITIONS AND PAPER are a part of a lot of magic. Petition papers usually are anointed with oils as part of the spell or ritual. When putting them in a substrate, it is strongly advised that you do not use oils as they can harm the root and poison your substrate. If you want to anoint the petition paper, the preferred method is to instead create a tea with the same herbs.

HERBS are a great addition to soil substrates and will decay over time like compost. You should avoid putting herbs in LECA semi-hydro setups and with sphagnum moss–based setups as they won't decompose fast enough and will invite molds.

WAX AND SPELL REMNANTS are always looking for a place to go when we are through with them, and a lot of witches feel weird about throwing them out. You can put them in your pots if you think the energy will be copasetic, but you should place them in a small glass jar before burying them. That way any toxic components won't leech into your soil.

Green Gnosis

PART SIX

Take a few moments to reflect on this chapter's text and then respond to the following prompts in your journal.

- *While raising indoor plants in the past, what soil- or substrate-related issues have you experienced? What do you think was the cause of these?*
- *What are three energies that you would like to bring into your magical workings with houseplants, and what aggregates would you work with to manifest them?*

Chapter Seven

Identifying Magical Correspondences and Properties

> [A]t my early age it seemed absolutely obvious that the church of the Earth was the greatest church of all; that the temple of the forest was the supreme temple. When I went to the sanctuary of the mountain, I found Earth's natural altar—Great Spirit's real shrine. Years later I discovered that this path of going into Nature, bonding deeply with it, and seeing Spirit within Nature—God, Goddess, and Great Spirit—was humanity's most ancient, most primordial path of spiritual cultivation and realization.
>
> John P. Milton, *Sky Above, Earth Below*

For the most part, we must approach hortocculture from the viewpoint of animism, where we recognize the inherent spiritual essence in all things, especially our plants. Identifying that essence helps us further explore concepts like correspondences and properties. Correspondences help us identify similar and parallel energies within two or more objects, places, people, or really anything capable of carrying a spiritual vibration. Properties, on the other hand, are the vibrational qualities present in those objects, places, people, etc. Honestly, I hate to admit it, but I have the perfect analogy; however, it requires superheroes, so bear with me.

Think of your houseplant as a superhero, any superhero. It can be one you already know or a totally different and undiscovered superhero that only you can see. It doesn't matter, just pick a superhero, this is already a little awkward for both of us. Properties are like their superpowers. They are the special preternatural qualities that give our plants the ability to do extraordinary things. Sometimes this superpower is love, sometimes it is protection or immunity from a specific type of danger, sometimes it is the ability to crawl into small places. There is a plethora of superpowers that our plants might have!

Correspondences, on the other hand, are more like the team members within the league of superheroes our plants belong to. Listed correspondences are all energy-transmitting, vibrational, unique superheroes in their own rights. They just happen to share a common goal, cause, or frequency, and we can work with one to get ahold of the other when needed.

Correspondences are used in magic to help us understand the spiritual relationship between one thing and another. They are a bit like schemas, a term more of you may be familiar with, which are essentially groups of things that are organized based on our cognitive perception and response to them. In occultism, correspondences basically help us identify parallel or equivalent energies and are used to help us not only make sense of how the metaphysical world works, but also how we might go about creating our own change within it. Once you understand how correspondences work, a lot of things start to make sense and you realize the "everything is connected" notion is really quite true.

Different spiritual traditions and customs provide different sets of correspondences, and while there certainly is a central idea around how we go about figuring out what corresponds with what, it is important to note that none of this is necessarily set in stone. While I would love to bore you with three hundred pages on how this whole notion of correspondences came about and how to hack the system, I will boil it all down to the finer points. And I share this with you not because I want you to throw all the correspondence charts in the wastebasket but because I want to remind you that you have a say-so in why something corresponds with something else. While I will share with you my correspondences to make this whole thing easy for you, they should be a starting point for you; your own gnosis about these things should supersede my own because it's *your* magic, not mine. This will all come in handy as you look at your houseplant collection and discover the magic within it. It will also come in handy when you inevitably end up falling in love with a plant and bringing it home only to find that it isn't listed in this book.

Identifying Houseplant Correspondences and Properties

Traditionally there are several factors that go into determining correspondences. I referenced schemas earlier because I think that term better fits what we are looking for here. To further explain, a schema represents the collected abstract knowledge that is stored in our memory, which helps us interpret information about people, places, things, events, etc.; think of it as the pipeline between the cognitive mind and our intuition. Identifying and codifying corresponding energy is a majorly intuitive process, and as you develop and assimilate more knowledge and wisdom, your ability to intuitively identify magical schemas will grow exponentially.

So, what exactly are we looking for here? What makes one plant mercurial and another Venusian? Well, it could be several things. It could be the color of the leaves, the pace of its growth, the time of year it flowers, the shape of the leaves, the mythology surrounding it, and so on. Basically, we look at the way it expresses itself and relates to humanity and then draw a comparison to another thing with it. Sometimes this is super easy, like with rose and its legendary correspondence with love. In this case, we have an actual Greek origin myth that says red roses come from the tears of Aphrodite and the blood of her lover Adonis. But even if we didn't have this myth, which is the case for almost all of our houseplants, we still have plenty of clues that would help us identify the rose as a plant associated with love.

Red roses are bold and fiery but possess a sweet floral scent and are highly prized by pollinators in the wild. The color red is associated with passion, the thorns are protective, the flower is abundant in petals, and the scent is alluring. We can take all of these clues and conclude that this plant would be aligned with the energies of love, which are passionate, protective, abundant, and alluring. While we won't be going into rose in this book, you certainly can grow it indoors as a houseplant with much success under the right lighting.

Let's dive into the methods and techniques employed by occultists throughout history to determine the metaphysical properties and correspondences of plants. These are the methods I used when developing my own practice with my houseplants and are the basis for the information I share on each plant later in this book.

Medicinal Properties

Normally this is a huge part of determining a plant's metaphysical properties. We turn to the plant kingdom for medicines, and it has taken care of us for thousands upon thousands of years; it is only natural that we would spiritually connect to the life-saving properties therein. With houseplants, however, that is a little tricky. Most houseplants are poisonous, at least a little, and few are known for medicinal properties. In the case of the plants listed later, only a small collection could be considered medicinal.

You can, of course, grow medicinal herbs in your home. Most medicinal herbs do well in windowsill boxes or planters and grow quickly, allowing for at least one or two harvests a year. I am a big fan of growing herbs that I can use medicinally and that I find myself frequently reaching for when casting spells. I find the herbs I grow work a little better than the ones I buy; it must be that whole "personal connection" thing. While there tends to be a strange divide between houseplant people and herb people, I would encourage you to try growing lavender (soothing to the nerves and great for the skin), sage (improves memory and purifies space), rosemary (antimicrobial and antiinflammatory, great for cleansing and releasing energy) mint (soothing to the body and stomach, cools tempers) and lastly garlic (immune boosting and protective). These all do great in the home and can be sprinkled into your other plants to help provide depth to your home design.

Now, all that being said, there are a handful of houseplants that *do* have medicinal properties! We will dive into each of these later, but if you are someone who is into the healing arts, you might want to take a look at the following three houseplants that are known to have medicinal properties.

ALOE VERA: This is one of those plants that I will be gushing all over in a few pages. My mother insisted on having an aloe plant in the house at all times to treat minor skin irritations and burns. It contains antibacterial, antiviral, and antiseptic properties and can be incorporated into a multitude of internal and external treatments. In magic we work with aloe to help heal the physical body, soothe the mind and temper, and help us work through self-destructive behavior.

TRADESCANTIA ZEBRINA (ALSO KNOWN AS SPIDERWORT): Many don't know that this easy-to-grow and popular houseplant has a long history of medicinal use in places like China, Malaysia, Mexico, and Jamaica. It is a common treatment for high blood pressure, hemorrhoids, kidney disease, irregular menstruation, and inflammation.[3] In magic we work with *T. zebrina* for matters of easing tension, moving through blockages, and releasing negative thought patterns.

NASTURTIUM: This beautiful, fast-growing plant is a fan favorite for many enthusiasts—and it happens to have one major medicinal profile! The leaves can be used to treat infection; when inhaled, steam from steeped leaves can help fight lung infections and bronchitis. The seeds can be ground into a paste and applied to fungal infections. In magic we work with nasturtium to assist in matters of exorcism, banishing, and restoring balance.

3 Gouri Kumar Dash, et al., "*Tradescantia Zebrina*: A Promising Medicinal Plant," *Indo Am. J. P. Sci*, 2017; 4(10).

Doctrine of Signatures

A method derived from ancient Greece and then popularized in several works on pharmacology, the doctrine of signatures states that plants resembling certain parts of the body have the ability to treat those parts. Eyebright, resembling an eye, is used to treat eye infections; lungwort, whose leaves resemble the shape of a lung, can treat the lungs; and toothwort, which has underground growth that look like teeth, is used to treat dental problems. Their magical properties all line up with their medicinal properties. In these cases, the folk names of the plant are clearly derived from the doctrine of signatures. Using our magical thinking caps, we can infer that the same technique can be applied to help us determine the magical properties of our houseplants. While there are thousands of varieties of houseplants on the market, there tends to be only a handful of shapes that we run into, with few exceptions. Let's take a look at the most common leaf shapes and what they tell us about a plant's magical properties.

HEART SHAPE: Probably the most common leaf shape in my collection, it can be found on philodendrons, anthuriums, alocasia, begonia, hoya, and others. For me, these leaves evoke love (all kinds), protection, and connection.

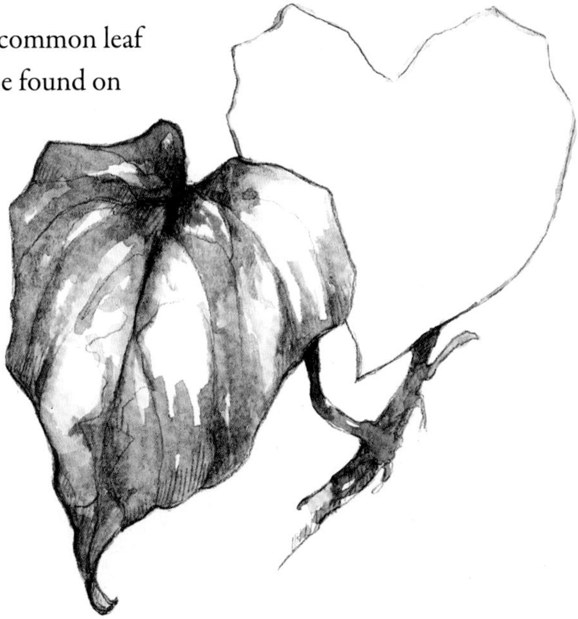

- ARROW SHAPE: Another common shape found often in immature plants like syngonium that I work with in magic when I need to send energy to a specific goal or target. I lean on these for spells I need to happen quickly.
- SWORD SHAPE: Just the pointy bit, not the hilt and handle. Leaves that jet out like long blades—such as those found in the agave or dracaena—are not only protective but also can be worked with in magic when you want a specific working to have an immediate impact on the surrounding environment. Great for workings that affect the home or office.
- SPATULA SHAPE: These are leaves that have a petiole that extends to form a broad leaf with a pointed end, such as the aglaonema and peace lily. These plants are great for getting energy to move and stir. I work with them in magic for change.

Other things that are along these lines to consider are growth rate, growth habit, and color and patterning.

Growth Rate

How fast or slow a plant grows also determines the type of energy it possesses. Plants that grow fast should be worked with for abundance, prosperity, love, protection, and pretty much anything you would like a lot of. I also turn to these for when I need a working to happen swiftly. Plants like tradescantia, most philodendron, and ceropegia are excellent companions for this type of work.

On the other hand, we might wish to work on long-term magic: things related to goals and planning, our families and career, our skills and hobbies, and we would most certainly turn to the slower growers for these things. Slower growing plants are usually hardier, stronger, and possess a longevity that faster growers do not. Plants like snake plants, bromeliads, and figs (*Ficus*) are great for these tasks.

Growth Habit and Lifecycle

This is where I have to restrain myself from showing you just how big of a nerd I really am. I have a particularly strong fascination with this topic and have devoted a lot of personal study to growth habits in my own plants. In my opinion, more than anything else, the way a plant grows tells us about its personality and metaphysical properties. In magic, growth habit will affect the way the work we do with the plant manifests in the world. It pertains to how the magic will form a path and respond to resistance. This is a major factor to bring into our overall equation. In each of part 2's plant profiles, I will reference its growth rate. Let's take a brief no-nonsense look at houseplant growth habits and what they imply about magical properties.

CLIMBING: While rooted in the soil, these are vining plants that latch onto structures (like moss poles, coconut coir, and wood) with arial roots. Their leaves mature as they climb, usually gaining in size and shifting in shape. In magic, I work with climbers when I need to be competitive, when I want my working to grow quickly and gain momentum, and as guides through the upper worlds. I also find these plants to be great partners when developing new skills and improving current ones. Additionally, I often turn to climbers for manifesting goals. Examples would be monstera, scindapsus, syngonium, and hoya.

SELF-HEADING: A form of climbing plant, self-heading plants are capable of growing upright, eventually forming a secondary leaf called a cataphyll that doesn't produce chlorophyll but instead is a protective structure for a developing leaf structure. We see this a lot with philodendron. They have larger, stiffer stems that are capable of holding the plant upright for years. They benefit from having something to climb on, but it isn't necessary. In magic I work with these as I would other climbers but also lean on them for protection and strength.

CRAWLING: These are plants that crawl out from a central clump and travel along the surface of the soil. Tradescantia, some philodendron, jasmine, and grape (*Cissus*) are all examples of plants with crawling habits. These plants perform excellently in hanging baskets and as companion plants in larger pots. In my magic, I turn to these plants to help find new ways of thinking, to find new paths and opportunities, and to push my magic out into the world.

CLUMPING: These plants grow outward and divide from a central plant, usually by developing corms, or offshoots, underground; think of grasses, alocasia, calathea, snake plants, some begonia, and ferns. I work with these plants mostly to impact the immediate surrounding area and find that they radiate energy outward in all directions quite well. This makes them ideal for home and hearth workings.

DENSE: These are plants that have a shrub-like growth pattern and tend to have a woody center. Primrose, cane begonia, and laurel are great examples. These are great plants to work with for complex magic where there are many parts that have to come together to get the job done. They make excellent companions when you are building something important in your life, developing new partnerships, and working in the astral.

MAT-FORMING: These are plants such as mosses and waterlilies that typically grow in moist and boggy conditions. They have creeping stems that branch out from a central point and form a mat-like cover. As these are excellent plants to calm and ground energy, many witches work with these plants in meditation spaces.

MOUND-FORMING: Mostly we see this with cacti and succulents. They are plants that grow to form a single round shape with offshoots forming aboveground. This is a particularly good way to reproduce where water is sparse. These are plants that I work with when preserving resources and, of course, for protection.

OPEN: These are plants that grow upward from a single stalk, trunk, or cane, resembling a dense habit but with fewer stems and a more open structure—think of bamboos and trees such as ficus. These are plants I partner with as symbols of the world tree when I am doing astral work as well as for strength and longevity.

Color and Patterning

You might have noticed that there aren't many flowering houseplants out there. There are orchids, desert roses, and a handful of others, but the majority of houseplants don't produce showy flowers. Some houseplants, like the common pothos, no longer have the ability to flower because they have been cloned so many times. Flowers also produce pollen, which most of us try to avoid due to allergies, so the majority of indoor plants on the market flower little if at all or produce little to no pollen when they do flower. When exploring houseplants and color, it isn't the flowers that we look to but rather the foliage (leaves).

The big thing to keep in mind when discussing foliage is that it exists to provide energy to the plant via photosynthesis, so foliage is always going to come in green to red hues as both can attract enough light to perform this task. A leaf couldn't be bright blue or yellow and produce photosynthesis. So, with houseplants we often get a wide range of greens, pinks, reds, and purples. That doesn't always give us a lot to work with in regard to color. However, where we lack in color diversity, we make up for in patterning! This patterning, which we call variegation, is responsible for some of the most sought-after houseplants on the planet.

Variegation will be something talked a lot about not only within this book but in the general plant market as well. Many plants are bred and cultivated for their variegation, so understanding how it works will be a useful tool moving forward.

Variegation is a pigment mutation that is being expressed by the plant, usually in foliage but sometimes in the flowers and stem. In most cases variegation is good, but one form of variegation, known as chimeral variegation, can be detrimental to the plant as it will inhibit the production of chlorophyl where it is present in the foliage. If you buy a plant like the *Monstera deliciosa* 'Albo variegata', *Philodendron erubescens* 'Pink Princess', or *Alocasia* 'Frydek variegata', which are all in-demand plants and likely will be for years to come, you will be responsible for not only keeping them alive but also for maintaining their variegation. Why maintain it if it is harmful to the plant? Well, not all variegation is harmful, and if it is, it doesn't have to be a life sentence. Chimeral variegation is the most common form of variegation; however, within the plants that carry this mutation, some of the rarest specimens on the planet can be found. If you properly care for them, these plants can live quite a happy and unique life.

To keep them alive, you will need a little extra humidity, a little extra light, and a little extra nutrients. Without the extra humidity the leaves are more likely to brown where they are missing pigment. This is especially true of 'Albo' and 'Aurea' variegation. The light and the nutrients are needed because it will grow slower than its non-mutated parent, and the extra nutrition can help make up for missing chlorophyl.

To keep a plant with chimeral variegation from reverting back to its non-variegated state, you will need to cut the plant back to a node/leaf where the variegation is strongest. This will cause the plant to activate a new growth point near the node, which will most likely carry on the stronger variegation. You should also take that as a sign that more light might be required to maintain the variegation in the future.

Unlike other forms of variegation, chimeral variegation may not pass down through its progeny. If a variegated plant breeds with another variegated version of the same species, there is no guarantee that the variegation will be expressed in the plants that grow from the seeds produced in this way. Instead, we must rely on root/bulb divisions or cloning.

In my magic, I work with chimeral variegation as a divination tool (see the varieomancy section in chapter 5). Each leaf has an entirely new pattern that can be gazed upon in meditation to help reveal hidden messages from the spirit world. I raise three plants specifically for this purpose, and two of them possess this particular form of variegation.

Green Gnosis

PART SEVEN

After reading this chapter's texts, take a few moments to observe the plants already in your collection. Choose up to five. Using the information provided here, create a magical profile for them based on your observations and feelings.

Chapter Eight

Perennial Pathworking

No risk is more terrifying than that taken by the first root. A lucky root will eventually find water, but its first job is to anchor—to anchor an embryo and forever end its mobile phase, however passive that mobility was. Once the first root is extended, the plant will never again enjoy any hope (however feeble) of relocating to a place less cold, less dry, less dangerous. Indeed, it will face frost, drought, and greedy jaws without any possibility of flight. The tiny rootlet has only one chance to guess what the future years, decades—even centuries—will bring to the patch of soil where it sits. It assesses the light and humidity of the moment, refers to its programming, and quite literally takes the plunge.

• • •

Hope Jahren, *Lab Girl*

The first year they sleep. The second year they creep. The third year they leap!

• • •

An old saying about perennials

Almost all houseplants are perennials, which means they have a lifespan that is generally several growing seasons, as opposed to annuals, which experience a full cycle within one growing season. Some perennials, like the giant redwoods (genus *Sequoiadendron*) here in the Pacific Northwest can live to be thousands of years old. The average life expectancy for a houseplant is somewhere between two to five years or more, and the entire time that plant will be in your care. It is perfectly reasonable for you to expect that with proper care and a deep bond, you can raise your plant for a very long time. I am not bringing all this up to frighten you away from houseplants but rather to let you in on a magical truth: Plants are capable of being fantastic companions in life and powerful allies in magic, but most importantly they can teach us a whole lot about ourselves.

Being part of our lives so intimately—I mean, we are literally bringing them into our homes—houseplants have unfettered access to very real parts of us that others don't see. They also come with massive ancestral knowledge. If we befriend them, include them in our lives as partners in manifestation, and turn to them for guidance, they use that ancestral knowledge to provide us with perspective and insight. While it is difficult to explain, it is possible to build a relationship with our houseplants that is deeply spiritual, deeply magical, and deeply inspirational.

As I have said in every other book I have written, the way to build a bridge to the spirits we seek is to spend time with them. With perennial houseplants we get to do this in some exciting ways that we don't normally get to with other aspects of our magic. Perennial plants go through stages of growth and dormancy as a response to the changing seasons. For most houseplants, this means that when winter comes, they either slow the production of new leaves to conserve energy or stop new growth altogether. Some will die back completely, leaving only a bulb or a few leaves. Once the season begins to shift, new growth continues—in most cases more vigorous than the last growing season.

Each part of this growth cycle contains its own magic and lessons to learn. Each phase of its growth shares a jewel of wisdom that we won't be able to find anywhere else. A big part of partnering with these plants involves us connecting to the wisdom and power of these moments. In this chapter I want to share with you some of that wisdom and power that I have personally received and how that has impacted everything from the way I live my life to how I practice my magic.

As you read, I want you to look at this as not just a bunch of fun metaphors coming together but rather as a pathworking that we are doing together. As we stop at each stage in the cycle to discuss gnosis and meaning, reflect and journal about what comes to mind in your own life. I want you to think about how the metaphors and stories apply to your own growth, and I want you to think about the houseplants in your life and what you think they might have to say about these stages. My hope is that as we do this, you will be inspired to think like a plant, if only for a while.

Dormancy

Plants have this funny way of keeping us honest that other elements of our witchcraft can't quite provide with the same consistency. As we grow, they grow. I find myself looking at plants that I brought into my home as unrooted cuttings that now reign supreme over entire areas of our floorplan and realizing that we have been through a lot together. With a little tender love and care, they went from tissue sample to royalty. I suppose if plants have taught me anything, it is that proper care can produce the most vivid colors and the strongest stems. What I mean by "they keep us honest" is just that; even if we don't feel like we are growing, we can see that they are. And, in a lot of ways, our houseplants are a reflection of who we are. So, one might say that their growth is proof of our own.

Now, I do want to loosely quote my friend Arin Murphy-Hiscock, prolific green magic author, who shared some wisdom in a workshop during an event I was hosting that has stuck with me pertaining to this very concept. Her workshop was titled "Wintering and Dormancy" (and between you and me, I wasn't super excited about it when she sent in the proposal; however, one does not make Arin Murphy-Hiscock pick another workshop, and I was just happy she said yes to the speaking invitation). It was, of course, an absolute hit. By the end of her workshop, my hand was cramping from writing up notes, and I was glad I hadn't asked her for another proposal! Anyway, the thing that has stuck with me is her saying (and I am paraphrasing here) that just because something isn't actively growing doesn't mean that it doesn't have potential or value. Those who aren't producing new growth all the time are just as important as the ones who are.

Friends, these words rang through me like a chime and landed somewhere deep inside that I didn't know was there. I honestly don't remember a thing about what she said after that because I just kept replaying those two sentences over and over in my head. Being someone who is constantly creating something, constantly working, constantly feeling like I need to produce the next thing, I very much needed to hear that, and I think some of you might too. I looked over at two mandrakes I was growing indoors who were still dormant from the winter and realized I needed to give myself—and them—a break.

While I still hold to my truth that our houseplants are reflections of who we are and how we grow, I have to hold space for what Arin said, and I think it helps me make my point about plants keeping us honest. For those of us who long for spiritual, professional, educational, and opportunistic growth, the idea of dormancy is uncomfortable, to say the least. But the truth is, it is a natural and necessary part of the cycle of growth. So honestly, is that slow period or stagnancy you are feeling in one area of your life or another really that bad of a thing? Is it worth getting stressed out and feeling helpless over? No. Probably not. It is a part of the cycle and will make for a bigger and better you when it is time to emerge, and it has no bearing on your potential or value. So give yourself a break!

Despite the fact that houseplants remain at consistent temperatures and that you may even have given them artificial lighting, many will slow down during winter months or go dormant altogether. Dormancy is more common in bulbous plants like elephant ears and could be an important part of the plant's growth cycle. Over the years there have been a few plants that I have had in warm grow tents with high humidity and regular sixteen hours of light a day and they still went dormant. Plants are smart, especially about taking breaks. If your plants receive any natural light at all, they will be able to tell seasonal shifts; the same goes for plants near windows that experience temperature changes and drafts. I actually prefer to lean in on this, reducing the amount of artificial lighting they get by 30 percent and watering most of my plants about half as much.

When our plants go dormant, allow them time to rest. I very much believe that at this time the indwelling spirits are mostly in the underworld, like Persephone. Sharing a bit of my personal gnosis here, my guides told me that during dormancy the plant spirit slips into a sort of shared dream with others of its kind. We can still access it if we need to, but it is best to let them take the time they need. The big lesson for me is patience and the value of rest, which are two things that I often find myself struggling with.

Now, let's say you are ready to emerge from dormancy and are eager to start the active growth process but aren't sure where to begin. Have no fear—plant medicine is here! Well, to be more specific, plants can show us how it's done. Part of working with the green flame is looking to the plant kingdom for advice and applying it directly to your life. That isn't always about meditating with a plant in your lap. No, more often than not, the real juicy stuff comes after learning as much practical information about a plant as I possibly can and then reflecting on how it survives this mad, mad world of ours in the wild. So let's look at a few houseplants that know a thing or two about dormancy and what they can show us about activating our growth.

When the weather gets colder and the nights become longer, most plants go through a process of dormancy where their active growth cycles shut down so they can conserve energy. Famously, many forests all over the world turn to gold and red hues as dormancy causes the vital fluids to pull downward toward the roots as a way of preserving the tree's most important parts. You aren't likely to see this type of dormancy happen with most houseplants. Instead, they either stop producing new leaves or new growth comes slowly. During dormancy it is important not to overwater houseplants as this can cause rotting. This is especially true for plants like elephant ears (alocasia, caladium, and colocasia), whose dormancy most often causes them to drop all leaves and dry up completely. When there is no active growth, overwatering is a real threat.

Elephant ears go into dormancy quite easily if they are not being watered enough or if they get too cold. A lot of people mistake this as the plant dying when, in fact, it is just going dormant. An easy way to tell whether your elephant ear is going dormant or dying is to gently squeeze the base/bulb with your fingers. As long as it isn't mushy, you are in the clear! Once all the leaves have dropped, you can withhold watering (a little here and there is okay), and in a few months it will try to come back when conditions are just right. You can also remove the bulb from the pot, dust off as much soil as possible, sprinkle it with a bit of cinnamon, and allow it to dry for a few days before placing it in a brown paper bag to overwinter. In the spring, repot the bulb, and you should be good to go!

Awakening from Dormancy

For the bulb to wake up, it needs to complete its cycle and really be ready to wake up—yes, that is the most important thing. The plant has to decide it is a good idea. You probably think I am totally off my rocker by saying that, but this is where we can really see that whole "plant intelligence" thing in action. Even if you provide everything it will need and make all the conditions just right, the bulb may just decide it wants an extra-long nap. So, the first thing we should recognize is that you have to be ready and want it, just like them.

The good news is that plants want to be alive! They want to live and thrive, so, generally speaking, they take every opportunity to do so, and chances are the bulb in question is ready, just like you. When conditions are right, coaxing them awake isn't all that hard, but keeping them awake can be. I have experienced more than one false-start, and every time it has been caused by not having everything I needed in place, including a decent plan. As the hortocculturist, your job is to give that bulb what it needs, just as being the witch, it is your job to give those stagnant areas what they need. In our case, instead of room temperature soil that gets plenty of indirect sunlight and weekly watering, we are going to need the right conditions for our unique task.

The first question to ask yourself at this stage is "What kind of substrate do I need to be successful?" Chances are a moist, rich soil is going to cause problems for you, even though that is what you think you need. Too much water and too many available nutrients can cause an emerging plant to die from rot or nutrient burn. While you will want these things later when you are at your peak, in the beginning these things might very well be too much. Don't jump in headfirst; instead, dip your toes in this whole "waking up" thing and take it slow to start. Overexposure could compromise your intentions and lead you into early burnout. Build up experience and know-how before fully committing.

The other thing to keep in mind as we drive down this highway of metaphor is it may not be safe to plant your bulb in one area or another; while we might really want to plant it where we think it will look the best, it very well may not thrive in that location, at least not in the beginning. So, where we put it is just as important as what we put it in. Sometimes our greatest anxieties stem from not feeling like it is safe for us to open up, so to ensure we are giving our metaphorical plant the best chance at new life, we have to ensure its safety. All this to say, in a not-so-metaphorical way: if it truly means something to you, make sure you feel safe in this new endeavor. This will provide you the best hope for immediate and long-term success.

This is the time to perform readings on your new endeavors and gain as much information as possible about what you can do to ensure your success.

Active Growth

Once we have emerged and set out our fresh foliage, we will soon enter a period of active growth. Through this stage of our development, we will be growing round the clock, day and night, but in different ways. As we continue to look to our plants for guidance, they have more than a few things to say about what we should do at this time and how to handle this whole growth process.

Like us, plants have a circadian rhythm that helps them distinguish night from day. In humans, this tells us when to get tired and rest and when to wake up, among other things. In plants, however, the circadian rhythm informs them on which type of growth they should be undergoing. We all know that photosynthesis is the process where plants absorb light to convert carbon dioxide into sugar and store it for use later. This can only happen during the day, and it is so important that plants spend most of their energy doing it while they can. At night, however, they consume those sugars through a process called respiration.

During respiration plants absorb oxygen and release a tiny amount of carbon dioxide through water vapor as they get busy putting all that sugar to use. It is at night that plants actually do most of their growing because they no longer have to spend so much energy photosynthesizing.

In our case, the situation is reversed. We sleep at night to restore ourselves and reserve energy, and during the day we spend that energy doing any number of things. But in the way that we can look to our plant's circadian rhythm to help understand how its growth is triggered, we can look at ours as well for the same insight.

As I sat in meditation over this one night, I was overcome with the realization that, especially as witches and magical people, our sleeping hours are filled with dreams and interactions with the spirit world. Even while our bodies are resting, our mind and soul are busy at work. Those dreams are both our subconscious processing the events of the day and our link to other worlds. The message that my plant guides shared with me that night is that we must cherish our downtime during periods of active growth and pay special attention to the dreams we have during these times, for they will reveal important messages about our efforts.

This was something that I thought was a no-brainer at first, but as I sat with it for a moment, I realized that it was a major issue for me and so many people I know. We think active growth looks like constant new foliage, but without meaningful rest there can be no growth.

On the flip side, we also need to spend our energy wisely when we are awake and working on the new foliage. Our actions must be intentional and we must grow with purpose; otherwise, we are exhausting energy—there is only so much that we are capable of producing and storing at once.

During this time there are no false starts, no need to tread too carefully unless you come up against resistance, and there is no need for you to diminish your capabilities. The only thing that matters is rest and respiration and maintaining the ability to do both.

Inevitably we will run into resistance or blocks during this stage, but luckily we have some pretty powerful allies to help us understand what to do. When a creeping or vining plant like pothos or monstera comes into something along its path that could be a block, it responds in one of two ways. The first is to grow around it and the second is to climb it.

Remember, there is only so much energy; every drop counts, so spending it working against blocks and resistance might not be the best use of this precious resource. Growing around it means that you are choosing to move beyond this limitation by taking a momentary detour. You are still growing outward and headed toward your intended destination, but you have had to make some momentary changes. No big deal—get back on the horse, right?

The second option comes when the block is too big to simply move around. When this happens, our plant friends go from crawling on the surface of the soil to climbing that obstacle. *Scindapsus*, *Philodendron*, *Epipremnum*, and others climb trees as a way of maturing and growing larger. They take the experience of adversity and use it to propel their growth. We could even go as far as saying that without moments of resistance, we wouldn't be able to mature ourselves.

When you enter a period of active growth, remember to use your energy wisely and rest with purpose. See adversity as an opportunity to mature, not as an impassible obstacle. You don't have anything to prove to anyone. Your only job is to grow and fill out your foliage.

Flowering and Fruiting

The ultimate sign that the active growth stage is a success is that from all of that green will emerge a flower, or inflorescence—something of beauty from your dedication and labor. It might be something tangible like a product or a piece of art, but it also might be an idea, something that inspires you to create something new or solve a problem. This is most often the case in my experience.

With flowers come pollinators, people who are drawn to that thing you have created. They bring pieces of other tangible things and ideas to the table and, as a result, will help to bring fruit to your work. Even when plants are capable of self-pollination, they still need a pollinator to shake things up or a gust of wind to release their pollen. This is the magic of collaboration and another valuable life lesson brought to us by plants. The fruits of our labor only come to pass when we work with others or if there is an act of the Goddess. To sell art, you need to work with a studio; to publish a book, you need an editor; to run a successful small business, you need distributors; and so on. Otherwise, you are left waiting for the wind to blow.

And look, I am aware of the exemptions to this rule and have seen plenty of people make it on their own, but even when they are their own boss and make all the decisions, they still have to collaborate with outsiders when taking their whatever-it-is to the next level. I can also tell you as someone who prefers to do most things solo, doing everything on your own is a miserable way to exist, especially as a creative person. It places all the pressure squarely on your shoulders and chokes the flowers before they even have a chance to unfurl. When you do unfurl that one flower that is able to make it, you realize that it is the only one in an empty field, with no one to see the results of your efforts and no one to help take it to the next level, praying for a miracle so that your flower can turn to fruit. It is okay to need other people; even plants need other plants.

Once our flowers are pollinated, the rest is all in the waiting for the fruit to mature and ripen. When they do, the plant will drop them, and inside those fruits will be tiny seeds that are ready to start their own adventures. Our plant, however, still has plenty of life left in it as a perennial! It will either continue to flower and fruit until the end of its season or it will prepare for dormancy by drawing its resources from the leaves back into the stem and roots, where it will wait until the time is just right for it to emerge and start again.

Green Gnosis

PART EIGHT

After reading each section of this chapter and reflecting, jot down any thoughts that come to mind regarding how each stage of the growth cycle relates to your own life. Next, reviewing what you wrote, describe how you will approach each stage in the cycle differently in the future and what has been successful for you in the past.

PART TWO

HORTOCCULTURAL *PROFILES*

Getting Planty

To such an extent does nature delight and abound in variety that among her trees there is not one plant to be found which is exactly like another; and not only among the plants, but among the boughs, the leaves and the fruits, you will not find one which is exactly similar to another.

LEONARDO DA VINCI

In this section I will endeavor to introduce you to several of my favorite indoor plant friends. If it were possible to list them all, you know I would, but that isn't in our cards so I have chosen the ones that you are most likely to run into when shopping for houseplants in big-box stores and nurseries as well as through online retailers. Entries are a mix of background and care information along with plants' magical properties and insights into working with their plant spirits when relevant.

I would like to reiterate that what I present here is my own gnosis based on my findings while personally working with each of these plants. There is no plant listed here that I haven't grown and worked with myself. I am not promising that I kept them all alive for longer than a year or two or that I didn't work with them for a while before passing them along to another planty witch friend, but I grew them, we were magical buddies, and they taught me a lot. It is my sincere wish that you will work with them as well and establish your own gnosis.

For the most part, each of the correspondences I discuss in this section come up in the first part of the book, especially chapter 7. There are one or two pieces of information listed in each profile that hasn't made its way to you yet, so let's cover those.

Care Level

I include care level to give you a bit of insight as to the level of difficulty these plants can have when caring for them. Easy plants like pothos, syngonium, aloe, and most succulents require little care and maintenance and can easily grow in all-purpose soil. These are harder to kill and are more forgiving with mistakes. Indoor plant hobbyists often joke that these plants thrive on neglect. Intermediate care–level plants like alocasia, aglaonema, and anthuriums require their own forms of specialized care, be it in the way they are watered, humidity requirements, or the sensitivity of the roots to standing water. These are plants that require regular attention and care. Advanced-level plants like some alocasia, begonia, and philodendron require even more care, with increased needs for their survival in your home. This is most often a light, humidity, nutrient, or water sensitivity. They will often require special setups like terrariums or similar.

Don't be afraid to try a plant out in the intermediate to hard range; just make sure you can provide the care it needs. Some of the most precious specimens in my collection are hard to care for, and I wouldn't have it any other way. The worst that could happen is that it dies and you learn a new lesson.

Toxicity

There are many houseplants that can be toxic to people and pets if consumed or if you come in contact with their sap. You shouldn't eat your houseplants or allow your pets to nibble on them. In some cases, like with ficus trees and hoya, the plant produces a natural latex that can be mildly poisonous if eaten or cause skin irritation; it could also be potentially life threatening to those who have latex allergies. Several houseplants also produce calcium oxalate raphides (crystals), which can cause irritation in the throat, eyes, nose, mouth, and skin, as well as gastrointestinal distress if eaten.

Just because we want a plant doesn't mean that it is a good fit for our home and those who live in it. If a plant is listed as toxic in this section, it means you should proceed with caution and do a little bit of extra research before you bring it into your home. You should also keep in mind that any chemicals you spray preventatively or put in the soil will also increase the likelihood of toxicity associated with your plants.

In general, I find there are a lot of people who feel conflicted about houseplants and potential toxicity with children and pets. I do not have children, but I do have a house full of pets, all of whom leave my plants alone. I achieve this by keeping my plants and their foliage away from spaces that are easily accessed by my pets. If something is face level to your pet, it is likely to take a playful chomp, so keep your leaves away from furry faces. I also spray my plants regularly with insecticidal soap, which makes them far less appealing to my pets. (I got some in my mouth one time on accident and it tastes worse than regular soap!) I keep plants on shelves and stools or hanging in baskets, and unless it is tall, like our sixteen foot bird-of-paradise, I keep them on some sort of platform whenever possible.

If you know you are working with a plant listed as toxic, it never hurts to wear a pair of gloves when taking cuttings or treating it. Many horticulturists believe we should be wearing gloves anytime we work with a plant for this purpose as well as to keep the spread of potential insects or sickness down.

Tarot

Tarot is a widely used form of divination with numerous possible applications. In my hortocculture, I work with tarot to help better understand my plants and help me make contact with the indwelling spirit. Tarot is listed here so that you can better understand the corresponding energies of the plants as well as so you have a bit of a shortcut in communicating with your collection. Work with the cards in meditation, readings, or as parts of a working.

If I mention something in this section that I didn't cover previously in the book, check out the glossary or index for clarification. Again, I recommend that if you come into the possession of a new plant, do a little research and find out as much as you can about it. In this section I often cover a genus and only get to discuss a handful of its species, or I write about a species and only get to cite a few of its cultivars. The chances of me hitting every plant on your wish list are slim; even all the plants on *my* wish list aren't profiled in this section. You know what? That is okay; there are a lot of plants out there, and we have already discussed methods that you can use to discern the magical properties of the plants you come across. Have faith, my green-thumbed friend, for we have prepared for that inevitability, and you are more than equipped to succeed where I have not.

Adenium

DESERT ROSE

Adenium is a rare gem in the succulent family that is an easy and sun-loving addition to any witch's garden. It is one of only a handful of plants grown indoors intentionally for its flowers, which are usually shades of pink in the wild but in cultivation come in a myriad of reds, whites, and pinks. Their flowers resemble those of the plumeria, which is a close cousin; however, the desert rose is uniquely prepared for drier conditions. It forms a caudex, which is a thick basal stem from which new growth emerges. The caudex helps with the reservation of water and acts like a trunk, allowing the desert rose to withstand harsh, dry conditions.

REGION OF ORIGIN: Africa and the Arabian Peninsula

GROWTH RATE: slow

HABIT: caudex succulent

DIFFICULTY LEVEL: beginner to advanced

GENERAL CARE: Adenium enjoys well-draining, sandy soil that is allowed to dry out during its dormant period (winter to early spring) and desires direct light. It requires little humidity. Propagate through seed or cutting. The cutting must be from the tip and allowed to callous for 24 to 48 hours before placing in water.

TOXIC: highly

VIBRATIONAL KEYWORDS: resiliency, hidden beauty, appreciation, joy

TEMPERAMENT: receptive

ELEMENT: earth, fire

PLANET: Venus

ZODIAC: Libra

MINERAL: rhodochrosite, jade, rose quartz, topaz

TAROT: Nine of Wands

AFFIRMATION: I will not just survive, I will thrive.

MAGICAL EMPLOYMENT: Adenium is a fantastic ally to work with when exploring mental and spiritual healing, when working on finding wholeness, when you desire to be appreciated, or when you want others to appreciate something or someone. In the bedroom it can help bring long-term relationships new energy. Near the front door it attracts new opportunities, especially for those with skills and experience who are seeking career growth later in life. Place it in the living/family room to increase joy and companionship among members of the house.

Aglaonema

CHINESE EVERGREEN

Aglaonema is one of my personal favorites, and many species do surprisingly well in lower-light conditions, making them ideal for places around the home that don't often get planty goodness. Typically they have spade-like leaves that jut out from a single stalk and are usually splashy or mottled with various shades of green, pink, red, yellow, silver, and even white. The foliage is some of the most colorful in the houseplant world, and specimens can grow to large sizes given time and attention. In Chinese culture it is associated with good fortune and luck and is a common plant to gift. There are well over two hundred species in cultivation, and more hybrids are released every year. They bloom in summer, but as a member of the aroid family, their inflorescence is quite boring and is usually removed to help the plant maintain foliage and reserve energy. It is one of the few plants that have actually made it into outer space and survived, and it has proven air-purifying qualities.

REGION OF ORIGIN: tropical and subtropical Asia and New Guinea

GROWTH RATE: moderate

HABIT: clumping

DIFFICULTY LEVEL: beginner to intermediate

GENERAL CARE: Aglaonema prefers well-draining soil and enjoys low to moderate indirect light but will thrive under bright indirect light. Higher humidity will produce larger leaves; however, most species do quite well in moderate to low humidity. Propagate by division or cutting.

TOXIC: yes

VIBRATIONAL KEYWORDS: luck, wealth, good fortune, new beginnings, resiliency

TEMPERAMENT: projective or receptive, depending on species

ELEMENT: fire, earth

PLANET: Jupiter

ZODIAC: Sagittarius

MINERAL: pyrite, jade, clear quartz, green moonstone, pearl

TAROT: Ten of Pentacles

AFFIRMATION: I appreciate my success.

MAGICAL EMPLOYMENT: Aglaonema is a fantastic ally to work with in matters of wealth, finance, and when coming back after setbacks. It is a particularly resilient plant, which gives it the ability to help us sort out our problems so we can find a way. As it grows and divides, so too will your prosperity. Placing one or more near your money altar will help spread its vibration throughout the home, and keeping one near the front door will invite new sources of income. In the bedroom it helps bring joy and excitement back into a relationship. When you gift an aglaonema, place three copper pennies that have been charged under the full moon inside the soil to bring cash into the person's life. Grow near where you do business and finance to help you get control over unruly spending and debt.

Species and Hybrids of Note

As I said earlier, I love aglaonema. There are so many varieties to choose from that it was difficult to create this small list, but in the end, there could only be eight.

A. Commutatum 'Silver Bay' has thinner leaves than other aglaonema that possess a stunning silver splash pattern all the way through the center. These are relatively easy to find and are particularly good at helping with matters of estate, business, and taxes.
CARE LEVEL: beginner

A. 'Sumatra' is a striped multicolored red, green, and gold variety with a reddish underside. It is sometimes called "Pride of Sumatra" or "Pride of India" and is adapted to growing in especially low light conditions. Its chocolate variety is one of the darkest aglaonema available. It is especially suited for shadow work surrounding financial matters.
CARE LEVEL: beginner

A. 'Siam Aurora', also known as "Siam" or "red aglaonema," is one of the most popular varieties in the West. It stays small in comparison to others and is loved for providing a splash of color year-round to indoor collections. This species is great to gift, especially to those in a new home, relationship, or business venture. Growing in the bedroom can attract new partners.
CARE LEVEL: beginner

A. Pictum 'Tricolor' is speckled with three tones of green. It is well suited for magic involving new business skills and entrepreneurship. Grow on a desk or in the office.
CARE LEVEL: intermediate

A. 'Wishes' is beloved by people the world over for its mostly pink leaves. This aglaonema is an excellent ally in business-related glamour magic and is great for those who speak in front of large crowds as it aids in eloquence.
CARE LEVEL: intermediate

A. 'Cutlass' has long, thin sagittate leaves with silver splashing. It is an excellent partner for clearing unwanted energies (like spite or jealousy) from the home.
CARE LEVEL: beginner

A. 'Frozen' is a green speckled variety with pink petioles. I have successfully worked with this when I felt creative blocks. I keep one next to my desk where I write just for this purpose.
CARE LEVEL: beginner

A. 'Valentine' is a popular aglaonema with dominant bright pink variegation throughout the leaf. This is an especially good partner in magic related to branding, public image, and social media.
CARE LEVEL: beginner

Alocasia, Colocasia, Caladium, Xanthosoma

ELEPHANT EARS

Alocasia, colocasia, caladium, and xanthosoma are all closely related members of the Aroid (Araceae) family that are collectively known as elephant ears. I love these plants so much that originally I was going to divide them up and give them each their own section, but in truth there is not enough that separates them from one another to warrant them each getting their own magical profile. As members of the aroid family, they produce unremarkable flowers with little pollen that bloom between spring and summer. They are grown, however, for their heart-shaped foliage, which can be large, colorful, and wildly patterned depending on the species. The larger alocasia and colocasia can reach great sizes; however, the most diversity in color comes from the smallest of the group, caladium.

REGION OF ORIGIN: tropical and subtropical Asia and Eastern Australia

GROWTH RATE: fast

HABIT: tuberous

DIFFICULTY LEVEL: beginner to advanced

GENERAL CARE: In general, elephant ears enjoy a well-draining but moisture-retentive soil, mid to high levels of humidity, and bright indirect light. They prefer temperatures in the 65 to 85°F range and may go into dormancy during dry periods. They are prone to pests. Propagate through division.

TOXIC: yes

VIBRATIONAL KEYWORDS: protection from unwanted attention, beauty, glamour, psychic development, divination

TEMPERAMENT: projective

ELEMENT: water

PLANET: Venus, Mercury, the Sun

ZODIAC: Taurus

MINERAL: rhodonite, shungite, amazonite, labradorite, obsidian

TAROT: The Empress, The High Priestess

AFFIRMATION: The beauty within is connected to the beauty that surrounds me.

MAGICAL EMPLOYMENT: Magically, they are protective in a defensive way, keeping us safe from unwanted attention and covetous energies. Keep them in high-traffic areas around the home, especially where company will be. In addition to their protective energies, elephant ears are also particularly posh plants that elevate the energy of the space they are in and can help project the energies of success. Don't work with them if you want to hide, however; instead, work with them when you want to be admired but not envied, respected but not feared, and loved for all your parts. Probably the coolest thing I like to do in magic with them is to use their leaves for divination, particularly the leaves of the colocasia and caladium. They make excellent surfaces to scry into and are often putting out new leaves, making them my go-to for almost all divination work.

ALOCASIA are unique in that they can grow to extremely large sizes over time; have thicker, sometimes leathery leaves; and prefer bright indirect light. They like chunky, well-draining soil and can tolerate drying up in between waterings. If anything, the concern with alocasia is generally in overwatering. They are similar in size to the colocasia; however, one way to tell them apart is that the alocasia leaves point upward and outward, whereas the colocasia point outward and down.

Alocasia Species of Note

While all alocasia carry the aforementioned energies, the following species make particularly potent allies and you are likely to run into them on the market.

A. 'Regal Shield' has large, thick, deep green, durable leathery leaves and makes an excellent companion when protecting property or the home from unwanted external forces. This variety does especially well in lower humidity as long as the soil doesn't dry out.
CARE LEVEL: beginner

A. amazonica 'Polly' (otherwise known as the African shield plant or the Amazonian shield plant) is an easy-to-care-for variety with silver veining that provides protection from the evil eye and theft. Keeping one near your computer will help guard against cyberbullying.
CARE LEVEL: beginner

A. macrorrhizos 'Stingray' is an epithet of the giant taro that has a thin tail-like structure on its leaf tip which makes the entire structure resemble a stingray! Capable of growing quite large (though the leaves are delicate), this species is great to work with when protecting yourself from negative thoughts and destructive behaviors. Its energy is all about self-restraint and keeping us from being our own worst enemies.
CARE LEVEL: intermediate

A. micholitziana, also known as *Alocasia* 'Frydek,' is a classic that always has me coming back for more! Its big velvety leaves are veined with white, creating stunning contrast and a thirteen-pointed pattern that resembles a primitive spirit drawing. I work with this alocasia for protecting family and friends and those I feel close to. Additionally, I find its plant spirit is always eager to communicate and participate in magic, so I recommend this one to anyone who might struggle to sense plant spirits.
CARE LEVEL: intermediate

A. baginda 'Dragon Scale' is a lower-growing alocasia that comes in a range of colors from deep green to light gray. The leaves are thick with dark veining and do indeed resemble what we might expect a dragon scale to look like. I partner with this variety specifically when protecting investments, valuables, and finances.
CARE LEVEL: advanced

COLOCASIA are similar to alocasia in almost every way except their leaves are thinner and they point downward from the petiole. They also prefer both more humidity and water, and they don't get quite as large as alocasia in most cases—the exception to this being *C. gigantea* 'Thailand Giant,' which can grow to have leaves that are up to four feet long. I was gifted one of these as a seedling, and by the end of its first year it was five feet tall. Most colocasia on the market are hybrids of *C. esculenta,* a midsize colocasia with suede-like leaves.

Colocasia Species of Note

I mentioned earlier that I turn to colocasia and caladium for divination purposes, specifically scrying. There are two colocasia in particular that I like to work with in this way.

C. esculenta 'Black Coral' produces black leaves that are big and beautiful and make the perfect planty substitute for a scrying mirror. Other black colocasia include *C. esculenta* 'Black Magic' and *C. esculenta* 'Black Ripple.'
CARE LEVEL: beginner

C. esculenta 'Mojito' has bright green to olive-colored leaves that are speckled with dark green. Because of its two tones and the patterning, I find these leaves to be particularly fabulous for divination. I connect them with the underworld and use the plant to communicate with the dead by asking them to send me messages in the leaves that I can discern.
CARE LEVEL: intermediate

CALADIUM are a lot like a more colorful, much shorter colocasia that enjoys similar growing conditions to an alocasia. They are usually sold as a shade plant in landscaping; however, they can thrive in the home. There are thousands of cultivars; many of them come from *C. bicolor* and are capable of producing some of the most vivid colors in all of the plant kingdom. I could do a book on caladium alone, but there is one in particular that I think you should keep an eye out for:

C. bicolor 'Burning Heart' is a slower-growing caladium that produces strikingly vivid solid red leaves. There are shades of red patterned over deeper red, and the whole leaf is really quite special. I work with these to help discern matters of the heart. You can name an emerging leaf after a lover and then once it has hardened off, you can use it to scry.
CARE LEVEL: intermediate

XANTHOSOMA are a bit more on the rare side as far as houseplants go, mostly due to lack of availability despite there being over seventy accepted plant species under this genus. Most common on the market is the *X. lindenii*, which is often confused for a caladium. In magic, working with the mature form of its leaves can help hide your psychic impression from others.

Anthurium

FLAMINGO FLOWER

Anthuriums are mostly epiphytic members of the aroid family and are a favorite among houseplant enthusiasts. Some anthuriums are grown for their inflorescence, while others are grown for their foliage. Anthuriums grow upward from a central stalk, producing offshoots from the base and dividing at the top when large enough. The leaves are almost always heart shaped. Anthuriums are popular houseplants all throughout the world, and while they prefer high humidity, most will do okay in average humidity. However, if you want to grow large anthurium leaves, then humidity levels between 70 and 85 percent are recommended. The flowers on the inflorescence are hermaphroditic, beginning as male and producing pollen, then maturing to female where they secrete a sticky liquid that catches pollen. There are around one thousand known species of anthurium; however, most of these are difficult to grow indoors without specialized environments. Anthurium was one of the plants tested by NASA's Clean Air Study and was shown to remove toxins such as formaldehyde and ammonia from the air.

REGION OF ORIGIN: tropical and subtropical South America

GROWTH RATE: moderate

HABIT: upright climber

DIFFICULTY LEVEL: beginner to advanced

GENERAL CARE: Anthurium like moist, chunky, well-draining soil as epiphytes and prefer high humidity with moderate to bright indirect light. They prefer temperatures in the 65 to 85°F range and may go into dormancy during dry periods. Propagate through division or seed.

TOXIC: yes

VIBRATIONAL KEYWORDS: love, loyalty, elegance, emotional protection, inspiration

TEMPERAMENT: projective or receptive, depending on species

ELEMENT: water, air

PLANET: Venus, Mercury

ZODIAC: Taurus, Gemini, Aquarius

MINERAL: golden healer quartz, citrine, sapphire, Herkimer diamond, topaz

TAROT: The Lovers

AFFIRMATION: My heart is full, and I have plenty of love to give.

MAGICAL EMPLOYMENT: Anthuriums are a favorite in magic, especially the rare ones that we will talk about next. In general, however, anthuriums seem to be incredible allies in matters of the heart and have a habit of drawing out positive vibrations wherever they go. The most common species is *A. andraenum*, also known as flamingo flower, which has rather plain traditional leaves but a colorful spathe surrounding the inflorescence. It can be found in a wide range of colors and sizes and makes a great beginner plant, especially for witches who want to filter negative vibrations from their home. Place anthurium in the bedroom to help remove negative patterns within romantic relationships. Grow it in high-traffic areas to help keep unwanted energies at bay and in the office or near the altar to help produce a feeling of sanctuary and calm. The plant spirit is particularly good at guiding us through the process of sorting out deep emotional trauma. Anthurium is odd in that it has both Venusian and Mercurial qualities, depending on the species.

Species and Hybrids of Note

Once you really get into houseplants and start looking beyond what you might find in the supermarket, rare and harder to find anthuriums are all the rage with enthusiasts, and for good reason: some of the harder to find varieties produce some of the wildest leaves you will ever place your eyes upon. Again, I wish I could list them all, but here are the ones that are easy enough to find online and in plant shops.

A. crystallinum is a beautiful subtropical variety that produces large, leathery leaves that are veined in silver, and the silver sparkles! The patterning is reminiscent of light reflecting on the bottom of a pool. There are now several hybrids of this species. It is particularly helpful when protecting the heart from emotional damage and easing depression. Tie a red ribbon around the stem with a new love interest's name to help ease jitters.
CARE LEVEL: intermediate

A. regale is similar to the *crystallinum*; however, its leaves grow much larger and produce more veining, and it has more distance between the septum. It is particularly good at protecting you during emotionally vulnerable situations as well as helping you form clear thoughts surrounding your vulnerability, assisting in shadow work.

CARE LEVEL: intermediate

A. forgetii has a similar silver patterning to the *crystallinum* but lacks a septum in its mature form, making it one of the oddest leaves in houseplant hortocculture. *Forgetii* is especially talented in matters of loyalty and makes an excellent plant to symbolize friendships. If you are worried about someone's loyalty, write their name on a piece of paper, burn it, and then sprinkle the ashes over the substrate and ask *A. forgetii* to reveal if they are being loyal to you or not.

CARE LEVEL: intermediate

A. clarinervium has a rounder leaf with a touching septum. It is usually darker than others and has light green veining. It is a great partner to work with on self-love and should be grown near a mirror to reveal inner beauty.

CARE LEVEL: intermediate

A. warocqueanum, also known as Queen Anthurium, produces long, leathery leaves that are veined with silver; mature specimens are true wonders of the plant kingdom. Grow to aid in matters of family, as it helps soothe generational discord and bring healing to generational trauma.

CARE LEVEL: advanced

A. veitchii, also known as King Anthurium, grows elongated, smooth leaves with bulging ripples that are reminiscent of abdominal muscles—only instead of a six-pack, our friend here is sporting a fifty-pack or more! *Veitchii* is a slow-growing ally who teaches us all about discipline and healing from self-destructive behavior.

CARE LEVEL: advanced

A. faustomirandae 'Faustino's Giant' can grow around five feet tall with large, thick leaves that touch at the septum. Work with it to cleanse the home and business of covetous energies and protect from the evil eye.

CARE LEVEL: intermediate

A. pedatoradiatum, also known as Anthurium Fingers, has leaves with deep fingerlike lobes. This anthurium is a great partner in work related to protecting the things and people that you love but cannot be physically present to protect. It is also an excellent partner in astral travel as it can assist in strengthening the tether between the body and soul.

CARE LEVEL: intermediate

Aralia

SPIKENARD

The Aralia family of plants are deciduous or evergreen shrubs, trees, and herbaceous perennials with a long history of magical application as they are all members of the Spikenard family. Spikenard is mentioned in the Christian Bible as Mary Magdalene is said to have used spikenard oil to anoint and cleanse Jesus's feet. There are around seventy known varieties of aralia, and the genus is constantly being updated. Aralias come in all shapes and sizes, but what makes them unique is that they have large clusters of double-compound leaves at the end of their stems. Sometimes the leaves are round and ruffled; in other species the leaves are bristly or feathery. While most aralias are toxic, *A. cordata* is actually cultivated as a food crop.

REGION OF ORIGIN: throughout Asia, Australia, and the Americas

GROWTH RATE: moderate

HABIT: tree- and shrub-like, sometimes rhizomatous

DIFFICULTY LEVEL: intermediate to advanced

GENERAL CARE: Aralias enjoy higher humidity but do well in normal conditions. They are considered an intermediate plant because of their watering requirements, as they prefer to be kept moist but not too wet or too dry. Once you get your aralia, keep an eye on it and adjust care accordingly for your environment. They require medium to bright indirect light and do not handle direct sunlight very well. They can be prone to leaf loss, but this shouldn't concern you too much as long as the stalk remains firm. If it gets mushy, you are likely to lose the plant.

TOXIC: yes

VIBRATIONAL KEYWORDS: intuition, spiritual exploration, psychic development, astral travel

TEMPERAMENT: receptive

ELEMENT: water, earth

PLANET: Moon

ZODIAC: Cancer, Scorpio, Capricorn

MINERAL: moonstone, moss agate, labradorite, chrysocolla

TAROT: The High Priestess

AFFIRMATION: My intuition leads me in the right direction.

MAGICAL EMPLOYMENT: Aralias are very interesting plants to work with in that the way they grow often makes them look like ancient trees due to their thicker stalks and peculiar-looking foliage. They give off the watery energies of psychic enhancement, making meditation and spirit communication easier to experience. On the other hand, they are earthy and bring stability to etheric frequencies, often making astral experiences more reliable and channeling sessions more dependable. Aralias are quick to respond to etheric changes in the atmosphere and are capable of dropping large amounts of leaves all at once as an early warning of major negative energy on the way. If this happens, pull back a bit on the watering and they will come back during their next growth cycle.

Species and Hybrids of Note

This is quite a large family, with several species capable of being grown indoors with little fuss. This genus is constantly being updated; species are being added to or removed from the list regularly, so fair warning that the plants here might be moved to another family. I have intentionally included two that have been removed but are still often sold as aralias.

A. 'Fabian' (*Polyscias scutellaria*) is a stumpy variety with small round leaves that have a green top and a purple-tinted underside. They are fantastic in temple spaces, near the altar, or around the house as allies to assist in focusing spiritual energies.
CARE LEVEL: beginner to intermediate

A. balfour (*Polyscias scutellaria Balfourii,* also known as *P. balfouriana*, also known as dinnerplate aralia) is similar to *'Fabian'* in shape, but its leaves grow larger and lack the purple tinting on the underside. It is particularly gifted at helping us with developing extrasensory perception.
CARE LEVEL: beginner to intermediate

A. 'Ming' (*Polyscias fruticosa*, also known as Ming aralia) has feathery leaves that make the plant look bushy and full. One of the hardier varieties, this aralia is a perfect addition to your collection if you attract unwanted spirit attention, especially during astral travel, as it helps to keep such energies at bay.
CARE LEVEL: beginner

Cyperus alternifolius, also known as umbrella plant, is a widely popular variety of aralia with oblong leaflets that emerge from the end of their stems and grow quite well in most conditions. Work with this plant when you want to conceal your magical workings, readings, and intuitive hits from others.

CARE LEVEL: beginner

Schefflera elegantissima, also known as *Dizygotheca elegantissima*, also known as false aralia, is similar in shape to the Ming; however, its leaves are elongated and spined. This is often sold as an aralia, though all schefflera were recently reorganized into a separate category. Work with this plant to aid in meeting spirit guides and plant teachers! Keep near sacred space in your home.

CARE LEVEL: intermediate

Hedera helix, also known as English ivy, is actually a member of the Aralia family and is a common trailing houseplant. It's a fantastic partner when performing astral travel, especially to the lower worlds, and should be grown to assist in the development of personal gnosis. It is also one of the most protective varieties of aralia, helping us remain hidden from those who wish us harm.

CARE LEVEL: intermediate

Polyscias guilfoylei has leaves that are toothed on the edges and can grow to around two feet tall. It makes an excellent companion when exploring the underworld and meeting new underworld allies. Additionally, it is a fantastic teacher for those wishing to explore their shadow side. It also can help attract ghosts and other spirits.

CARE LEVEL: intermediate

A. japonica (*Fatsia japonica*) is an aralia with large elongated leaves that have up to eight lobes. It can grow upwards of sixteen feet tall, given enough time. Grow *japonica* when you want to remove and filter negative astral and etheric energies from the home. Note this is safe for pets, whereas the others listed here are not.

CARE LEVEL: beginner

Araucaria heterophylla

NORFOLK ISLAND PINE

Reminiscent of something we might see in a dinosaur movie, the Norfolk Island pine is a coniferous tree endemic to a small island off the coast of Australia. It has a straight trunk with branches that grow symmetrically, producing an overall triangle shape, making it quite appealing to the eye. When it matures, the leaves change from being thin needles to thicker needles that point upward, giving it the name *heterophylla*, or two-leaved. As a slow grower, it makes a great houseplant; while in the wild it can grow up to two hundred feet tall, yours will likely only grow to a fraction of that.

REGION OF ORIGIN: Norfolk Island, Australia

GROWTH RATE: slow

HABIT: tree

DIFFICULTY LEVEL: beginner to intermediate

GENERAL CARE: Norfolk Island pine is one of the few houseplants that prefer higher levels of light, including a few hours of direct sunlight if possible. Water thoroughly and allow soil to dry out about 25 percent between waterings. In the winter, increase humidity and decrease watering by about half.

TOXIC: yes, mildly

VIBRATIONAL KEYWORDS: wisdom, order, cleansing, protection

TEMPERAMENT: projective

ELEMENT: fire, earth

PLANET: Saturn

ZODIAC: Capricorn

MINERAL: moss agate, bloodstone, sodalite, nuummite

TAROT: The Emperor

AFFIRMATION: I am here for the experience.

MAGICAL EMPLOYMENT: Many witches work with pine trees and their cones in magic for fertility and prosperity, which the Norfolk Island pine can certainly help you with. It can also be a lifelong tree teacher who mentors you in the ways of spiritual clarity, spiritual cleansing, and spiritual protection. It is also an excellent plant to include in workings for Pan, the Green Man, the god Saturn, and any other form of the divine masculine.

Arecaceae Family

PALMS

The Arecaceae family is known by its large compound leaves that emerge from an unbranching stem. There is still a lot of studying to do with these plants, but at present there are some twenty-six hundred varieties growing in habits ranging from climbing to treelike, with the first species appearing in the fossil record around eighty million years ago. Palms come in many shapes and sizes, and several of them do quite well in an indoor setting. There are several species from other families that commonly get misidentified as palms, especially dracaena. Palms primarily have two types of leaves: those that are fan-shaped and those that are referred to as "feather-leaved," which are thinner and more compound around the top of the stem.

REGION OF ORIGIN: tropical and subtropical climates globally

GROWTH RATE: slow to moderate

HABIT: climbing, shrub, or tree

DIFFICULTY LEVEL: beginner to intermediate

GENERAL CARE: They enjoy moist, well-draining soil and high indirect and direct light. While most sold for indoor use are tolerant of lower humidity, they prefer humidity at or around 50 percent or higher.

TOXIC: Most are not.

VIBRATIONAL KEYWORDS: peace, relaxation, sanctity, spiritual balance, luxury

TEMPERAMENT: projective

ELEMENT: water, earth

PLANET: Venus

ZODIAC: Pisces, Cancer, Taurus

MINERAL: serpentine, atlantisite, chalcedony, chrysoprase, blue calcite

TAROT: Four of Swords

AFFIRMATION: I like the feeling of having enough energy.

MAGICAL EMPLOYMENT: Palms unite water and earth energies in a very Venusian way: through beauty and relaxation. They are peaceful plants whose slow growth and tendency to be solo teach us lessons related to balance and patience. We can grow them to attract wealth and luxury, and they make excellent additions to glamour and love spells. I turn to palms to help create a feeling of sanctuary and often incorporate them in workings related to connecting with Mother Nature.

Species and Hybrids of Note

There are more palms than I could ever fit in this section, but here are a few that I have partnered with in magic over the years that stand out as allies you also might like to get to know. Those listed here are safe for pets.

Livistona chinensis, also known as the Chinese fan palm, is a classic houseplant whose leaves fan out with spikey fingers. These are often seen in movies where someone is fanning a sexy beachgoer, and they can be dried and used in crafts. Work with these to cool tempers and inspire resolutions to problems.
CARE LEVEL: intermediate

Chamaedorea elegans, also known as the parlor palm, is a highly popular species that can grow to around sixteen feet tall. Its soft leaves and ease of care make it ideal for growing in the home. Work with it to help build a calm space and learn valuable lessons about self-care.
CARE LEVEL: intermediate

Dypsis lutescens, also known as the Areca palm or butterfly palm, is similar in appearance to *C. elegans*; however, its leaves are sturdier and not as herbaceous. It is a good air-purifying plant and can be worked with in magic to remove negative energies from spaces.
CARE LEVEL: intermediate

Aspidistra elatior

CAST-IRON PLANT

This classic houseplant has lance-shaped green foliage and is known for being one of the best plants for beginners because it is so hard to kill! It is capable of withstanding low light and temperature changes, and it doesn't require any special humidity. While it typically doesn't flower indoors, it is possible to do so. The highlight for most is the glossy finish to the foliage, which can grow up to two feet in length. Interestingly enough, it is actually related to asparagus; however, while it is not toxic, you probably shouldn't eat your cast-iron plant.

REGION OF ORIGIN: southern Japan

GROWTH RATE: slow

HABIT: rhizomatous

DIFFICULTY LEVEL: easy

GENERAL CARE: Prefers well-draining soil and being kept moderately moist, but other than that it does not have too many needs. Like most plants, it benefits from higher humidity and warmer conditions, but it is happy as long as conditions don't drop below 50°F. Propagate through rhizome division.

TOXIC: no

VIBRATIONAL KEYWORDS: longevity, limitations, rebellion, coalescence

TEMPERAMENT: projective

ELEMENT: earth

PLANET: Saturn

ZODIAC: Aquarius, Capricorn

MINERAL: smoky quartz, obsidian, jet, atlantisite, sapphire

TAROT: The World, The Devil

AFFIRMATION: The world I create for myself is beautiful.

MAGICAL EMPLOYMENT: The cast-iron plant is an interesting one to work with in that it is very much about survival and longevity and can teach us a lot about living safely in our environment. Because of this, I often turn to it for magic regarding children. You might be looking at the tarot and planetary associations and be thinking I am off my rocker, but I do this because boundaries aren't bad; sometimes Saturnian energy can provide a stable foundation for great things to come. On the other hand, it is also a plant we can turn to for assistance in matters where we need to resist something.

Begoniaceae

BEGONIA

There are over two thousand species in the genus *Begoniaceae*, and sorting them all out can be a bit cumbersome. We generally divide them into smaller groups based on their growth habit. Three of those are often seen as houseplants: rhizomatous, rex, and cane. The other two categories, wax and tuberous, are most often grown outdoors and are generally considered landscaping plants. Begonias have a huge range of color—from black to bright pink to purple—and some even produce a blue flash when under bright light. Blue, by the way, is one of the rarest colors in the plant kingdom.

The foliage can be striped, polka dotted, bullate, ribbed, furry, and just about every combination of those things. What unites them is their flowers and a shared genetic makeup. Being monoecious, they have both male and female flowers on the same inflorescence. In some species the flowers are quite bright and colorful, with relatively plain foliage, and in others the inflorescence is understated while the foliage showcases vibrant colors and patterning. Wildly popular as houseplants, if you are looking for color, begonias are the place to start! I will also add that if you are interested in restoration and preservation, there are many begonias available in cultivation that are extinct or endangered in the wild. Private collectors all over the world are working to save many of these species, and you can participate, too.

REGION OF ORIGIN: subtropical and tropical regions worldwide

GROWTH RATE: moderate to fast

HABIT: several

DIFFICULTY LEVEL: beginner to advanced

GENERAL CARE: All begonias enjoy loamy, well-draining soil that is allowed to dry out just a bit between waterings. A soil mix of 50 percent potting mix to 50 percent small perlite is great for most species. I let mine go without water until I see the leaves start to droop before watering the pot completely. This encourages growth of their delicate roots. Do not allow water to accumulate, however, as begonia are sensitive to root rot. They require low to bright indirect light, depending on the species. Propagate from leaf (and sometimes stem) cuttings. Most begonias make excellent terrarium plants. I recommend checking out the individual care needs of the begonia you are purchasing prior to committing, especially if you are buying a rare species.

TOXIC: yes

VIBRATIONAL KEYWORDS: creativity, passion, energy, sexuality

TEMPERAMENT: projective

ELEMENT: fire and other elements depending on species

PLANET: Mars

ZODIAC: Aries, Leo, Sagittarius, Scorpio

MINERAL: fire agate, lapis lazuli, topaz, garnet, peridot

TAROT: Knight of Wands

AFFIRMATION: I manifest my desires onto this plane with ease.

MAGICAL EMPLOYMENT: Begonias have a very fiery energy to them that always enjoys being invited into magical practice. I have around thirty different species, and each of them seems to be a blend of fiery energy and something else, all depending on their color and growth habit. Begonia energy isn't aggressive, but it is excited. In general, begonias are great with creativity, especially when it can come in the form of art or writing.

Species and Hybrids of Note

Let's take a closer look at the growth habits of the begonia family and dive into the special magic each of them is capable of.

RHIZOMATOUS BEGONIAS have large, colorful leaves that emerge from a thick rhizome that crawls along the surface of the substrate. Some varieties can grow to have leaves that reach up to three feet in diameter. They do well in shallow containers and can spread quite quickly when given the space during their growth season. Magically speaking, the rhizomatous begonia is special in that it grows close to the ground and is the earthiest of the genus. It is particularly good at helping create practices and skills that ground your dreams and can attract opportunity for new skills into your life. While I would love to share my top ten, here are three that stick out in my mind especially for witches.

B. 'Tiger Kitten' is a small-leaved variety with deep green leaves that are splashed with neon. It is great for all things education and training and should be raised near your desk to assist in memory retention.

CARE LEVEL: beginner

B. 'Betsy' is an iridescent blue and green species that might require a terrarium in your home's conditions. It is truly gorgeous and flashes blue in bright light. It is especially good at creative endeavors where you want to get attention, and it is also great for helping sculpt public image.
CARE LEVEL: intermediate

B. melanobullata is a rare species with broad green leaves that are speckled with black, furry spikes. It not only looks witchy as can be, but it truly vibrates with the energies of the underworld. Work with it when developing psychic abilities, communicating with the dead, and for assistance when tapping into your witch power.
CARE LEVEL: advanced

REX BEGONIAS are hybrids descended from a particularly large variety of rhizomatous begonias from India called simply 'Begonia Rex'. While they are rhizomatous, their size, even among that genera, is quite spectacular. In your magic, rex begonia are excellent partners in manifestation. Since I can only pick three, I think witches will especially find these species to be of interest.

B. rex 'Escargot' has bicolor green leaves that form in the shape of a clockwise spiral, resembling a snail. I recommend working with this begonia in your meditation space and growing it near the front door to attract desired energy. It is excellent to keep around altars as the invoking shape of the foliage is quite inviting to deities.
CARE LEVEL: beginner

B. rex 'Rumba' is a red and black variety with velvety leaves that is particularly attuned to romance and sexuality. Work with this to attract sexual partners and when exploring your sexuality, as it helps make us more comfortable in our own skin.
CARE LEVEL: intermediate

B. rex-cultorum is a vibrant, wildly colored, and popular begonia that is known for its green, silver, red, and purple hues that are different in each leaf. It is the parent of many hybrids and has been in cultivation since the 1850s! If you have big dreams and aren't sure how to make them into reality, cultorum varieties can help with that. They are great at helping us build confidence and navigate the landscape of manifestation.
CARE LEVEL: beginner

CANE BEGONIAS, also called angel wing begonias, are an upright clumping variety that host a range of leaf shapes, and most often the leaves do resemble a pair of wings. In magic these begonias are excellent partners when communicating with divinity, muses, and higher-vibrational spirits. There are over eighty registered species and over one-thousand cultivars of cane begonia, and while I would love to talk about all of them, these are my favorites.

B. maculata 'Wightii', also known as the polka dot begonia, has large dramatic green leaves that are dotted with silver. It makes an especially good companion for strategizing and planning the real-world elements related to achieving our goals.
CARE LEVEL: beginner

B. 'Lucerna' has dark olive-colored leaves that are speckled with silver and are red on the underside. It is a fantastic plant of the Muses and should be worked with for inspiration and creativity. It also happens to be a particularly fast-growing variety that is relatively easy to care for.
CARE LEVEL: beginner

B. 'Looking Glass' is a stunning cane species that is predominantly silver. I work with this variety to communicate with angelic beings and ancestors, and I recommend growing it near the back door to anchor those energies in your home.
CARE LEVEL: beginner

Bromeliads

AIR PLANTS

Bromeliads are a large and complicated family of plants that are considered to be one of the more recent groups to have developed. They have specially evolved to live in conditions where soil is poor and are capable of living in a wide range of possible habitats thanks to this adaptation. Some are epiphytes, some are lithophytes, others are terrestrial, and the family shares a range of leaf shapes that goes from large and broad to needle-like. There are currently eight subfamilies in this family; however, we are only going to be focusing on two of them as they are the most common in the houseplant market: Tillandsioideae and Bromelioideae. Both have their own special needs and magical properties, but all bromeliads assist in the mental and creative elements of magic. In addition to these traits, they are also some of the easiest plants to take care of once you understand them, so I highly recommend keeping them in your collection if you get the chance.

REGION OF ORIGIN: all over the Americas

GROWTH RATE: slow to moderate

HABIT: epiphytic and terrestrial

DIFFICULTY LEVEL: beginner to advanced

GENERAL CARE: see individual description for care

TOXIC: no

VIBRATIONAL KEYWORDS: thought, inspiration, communication, justice

TEMPERAMENT: projective or receptive, depending on species

ELEMENT: air

PLANET: Mercury

ZODIAC: Libra, Aquarius

MINERAL: kyanite, kunzite, morganite, aquamarine, fluorite, clear quartz

TAROT: Ace of Swords

AFFIRMATION: My thoughts become reality.

MAGICAL EMPLOYMENT: see below

Species and Hybrids of Note

This hugely popular family is diverse and there are many options available on the market today. Let's take a closer look at the growth habits of the bromeliad and dive into the special magic each of them is capable of.

TILLANDSIODEAE (also known simply as tillandsia or true air plants) is a subfamily that has over six hundred and fifty known species that can be found all throughout the Americas. These are special in that most require no substrate to live, instead choosing to draw moisture and nutrients from the air through rain, dust, decaying insect matter, etc. In the wild they grow as epiphytes and aerophytes and can be seen growing on everything from house siding to telephone poles. In the home they can be tricky because they love humidity and can easily dry out, so regular misting is required along with a weekly water dunk. In magic they are incredible partners for those of us who live a creative lifestyle, as they can literally draw everything they need from the air. If you seek inspiration, these are the plants for you! Let's take a look at three easy-to-find species that can level up your magic.

T. usneoides (also known as Spanish moss) thrives in the humidity of the Southern United States and South America. In addition to looking fantastic draping from hanging baskets and in terrariums, it also makes one heck of a magical shield when grown in abundance. Even the tiniest bit, however, can be grown to aid creative thinking and problem solving.
CARE LEVEL: beginner

T. xerographica is a curly leafed variety where leaves emerge from a very small and bound central stalk. It is iconic and highly sought after by collectors for its medusan look and potential size. Work with it in magic to increase mental focus and for concentration.
CARE LEVEL: beginner

T. ionantha, with its colored tips, is probably the most popular variety of air plant on the market and is often glued to rocks or shells and sold at pet stores. This variety is an excellent companion for those who write music.
CARE LEVEL: beginner

BROMELIOIDEAE (also known simply as bromeliads) are the namesake of the whole family and make up a huge portion of what we see on the market. Unlike tillandsia, bromeliads do require substrate; however, they are adapted to drier conditions, even developing a way of storing water between their rigid leaves called the "tank method." Their special leaves create small pools of water that allow them to absorb it slowly and that act as homes for insects and their larvae, which in turn enriches the water. In this family we see some of the most colorful displays in nature and one of the sweetest.

Ananas comosus (also known as the pineapple) is a spiny bromeliad that slowly produces a sweet edible fruit that tastes great in a daiquiri. These are surprisingly easy to raise indoors, but their growth is hindered compared to their outdoor family. Raise them to assist in long-term creative projects as they help us remain patient. They can also be raised to increase happiness, especially related to otherwise menial tasks.
CARE LEVEL: beginner

Aechmea chantinii is a large broad-leafed bromeliad with silver splashing or stripes. It is especially well suited for busy, creative places like offices or studios, where it helps in team building and bringing focus.
CARE LEVEL: beginner

Neoregelia carolinae is a vibrant and smaller growing bromeliad known for its red and pink hues. This is especially great to work with for those working in the visual arts, those seeking to inspire creativity in the bedroom, and those who want to bring attention to their creative endeavors.
CARE LEVEL: beginner

Carnivorous Plants

FLYTRAPS, SUNDEWS, PITCHER PLANTS, ETC.

Okay, so this is cheating a bit, but I wanted to make sure these were included, and I thought giving them one big entry would work best as a group. Carnivorous plants are an unrelated group of specialized plants that have evolved to survive in regions with poor substrate quality by developing various ways to eat insects and, on occasion, small animals. Some species have even evolved to harvest the dung of rodents who lick a sweet honeydew that forms on the lids of their trap. Some have specially timed mechanisms that spring shut, trapping their prey within a modified forked leaf. Others are just sweet and sticky, acting like flypaper and waiting for their prey to land. What makes them special beyond their taste for flesh is that energetically they bridge the worlds of flora and fauna as the only plants to survive this way.

Carnivorous plants are very primitive in their own way. They don't grow terribly large, they don't spend a lot of time making roots because they don't really need the soil, and even the way they capture prey is simple and effective. What energy they do have is mostly spent on growing traps and foliage or making flowers for reproduction. Compared to a lot of other plants in this index, they are relatively simple.

While they are not your typical houseplant, recently they have become more popular as people discover newer ways of providing for them. Around 583 species are classified as carnivorous, but there are only a few that do well in the

home without a lot of extra effort, so I am going to focus on the ones that are proven survivors with proper care. They should receive rain or distilled water as they are sensitive to chemicals, and they should never receive fertilizer.

REGION OF ORIGIN: tropical to temperate regions globally

GROWTH RATE: moderate

HABIT: multiple

DIFFICULTY LEVEL: intermediate to advanced

GENERAL CARE: Require high light, distilled water, and a moss or peat blend containing up to 50 percent perlite. Do not fertilize.

TOXIC: Most species are.

VIBRATIONAL KEYWORDS: protection against magic

TEMPERAMENT: receptive

ELEMENT: fire

PLANET: Venus, Mars

ZODIAC: Aries, Leo, Sagittarius

MINERAL: black obsidian, charcoal, hematoid quartz, shungite

TAROT: King of Wands

AFFIRMATION: Evil fears me.

MAGICAL EMPLOYMENT: Carnivorous plants can offer us something in our practice that no other type of indoor plant can while alive: protection from magical attack and malicious spirits. Their propensity to prey upon pests makes them ideally suited for this task, and I have found their plant spirits eager to help when asked.

Species and Hybrids of Note

While they are all capable of protection, there are five carnivorous plants that I would like you to meet if you get the chance.

Dionaea muscipula, also known as the Venus flytrap, is likely the variety you are most familiar with. They have modified leaves which form snap-traps that are triggered by tiny hairs inside. Once the insect stimulates one of the hairs, the trap shuts and seals the prey inside, where it is slowly digested. These plants require high humidity, so a terrarium of some kind is recommended for best results. They mostly grow in peat.

Sarracenia is a genus of plants with upward-pointing, bell-shaped pitfall traps. Insects find themselves slipping into a well of digestive liquid that is difficult to escape. They mostly grow in peat and come in a selection of colors and patterns that range from green to red and white. You can grow them in a bog-like setup where you submerge their pot halfway in a large bowl of water. Interestingly enough, they can be susceptible to spider mites.

Nepenthes, also known as pitcher plants, produce large, colorful, and sometimes intricately patterned bell traps on the end of smooth (and sometimes furry) leaves. They make great hanging plants; however, some species can grow to several feet tall. They need to be planted in a 50/50 mix of sphagnum and perlite as any organic potting mix can cause them to stop producing bells or even die.

Drosera, also known as the sundew, produces filament-like leaves with sticky hairs that lure insects before folding in on them and trapping them. It does not like to be touched, but it is fun to watch in action and makes for a fast-acting magical ally.

Pinguicula, also known as the butterwort, is similar to the drosera but its leaves are broad and it doesn't fold up to trap its prey. Instead, it acts like flypaper and digests prey that become trapped right there on its leaf.

Chlorophytum
SPIDER PLANT

Chlorophytum, commonly known as the spider plant, is easily one of the most recognizable plants on the market and in homes. It has long slender leaves that grow in a rosette and sends shoots out with plantlets on the end that eventually will take root when they touch the soil's surface. These shoots look like legs, giving it a beastly appearance and the inspiration for its common name. They make excellent hanging plants because of this interesting growth habit, and as a genus they are generally hardy and capable of withstanding a multitude of growing conditions.

REGION OF ORIGIN: Africa, Australia, Asia

GROWTH RATE: moderate to fast

HABIT: clumping

DIFFICULTY LEVEL: beginner

GENERAL CARE: They prefer regular potting mix and like to be thoroughly watered once the soil has become 50 percent dry. Propagate by cutting off plantlets and letting them root in soil.

TOXIC: no

VIBRATIONAL KEYWORDS: prosperity, abundance

TEMPERAMENT: projective

ELEMENT: earth

PLANET: Venus

ZODIAC: Taurus

MINERAL: citrine, pyrite, peridot, malachite, jade

TAROT: Six of Pentacles

AFFIRMATION: There is enough to go around.

MAGICAL EMPLOYMENT: Chlorophytum is an easy money plant to work with that you should hang near cash registers, windows of businesses that don't receive direct light, and anywhere you associate with finance. Its propensity to grow quickly and put off plantlets make it ideal for this type of magic, and the plant spirit seems content on helping with those matters provided you treat the plant well.

Codiaeum
CROTON

This is a fun one to explain. The name *croton* is used commonly for the plant *Codiaeum variegatum,* which is a succulent-like subtropical evergreen belonging to the Euphorbia family. It is also the name given to an entirely different subgroup within the same family, which does not include the common croton. For our purposes, we will be discussing the common croton (*Codiaeum variegatum*). These are hardy and beloved by many collectors because they remain colorful year-round and are tolerant of irregular care. Their foliage is small and ovate and is either speckled or striped with red, yellow, orange, and green, depending on the cultivar. Like begonia, they are monoecious and capable of self-pollination.

REGION OF ORIGIN: Malaysia, Australia, Southern India

GROWTH RATE: moderate

HABIT: shrub-like

DIFFICULTY LEVEL: beginner

GENERAL CARE: All-purpose soil works well for these. Avoid letting them stand in water for longer than necessary, and avoid temperatures below 40°F. Propagate through stem cutting.

TOXIC: yes

VIBRATIONAL KEYWORDS: imagination, acceptance, persistence

TEMPERAMENT: projective

ELEMENT: fire, earth

PLANET: Saturn

ZODIAC: Capricorn

MINERAL: jasper, garnet, aragonite, tiger's eye, malachite

TAROT: Nine of Wands

AFFIRMATION: I am exactly where I am supposed to be exactly when I am supposed to be here.

MAGICAL EMPLOYMENT: Croton is a great ally in the war against imposter syndrome, as its bright colors and eagerness to fill whatever niche you put it in makes it a comparable teacher in these matters. Work with croton to help find your place in family and community; turn to it for advice on how to love what makes you different. It teaches us how to be strong in the face of adversity and encourages us to step into the total potential of our being.

Coffea

COFFEE PLANT

We all know and love coffee, but did you know a lot of people grow it as a houseplant? Well, now you do. This was actually a surprise to me when I got hardcore into houseplants, and it immediately became a favorite of mine. The plants grow as a shrub that can, with much time, grow upward of seven feet tall. They produce beautiful small white blooms that can be pollinated, possibly leading to the formation of a coffee bean. It is possible to harvest enough beans from a three- to four-year-old plant to make your own pot of dark, delicious goodness.

REGION OF ORIGIN: Africa

GROWTH RATE: moderate

HABIT: shrub

DIFFICULTY LEVEL: intermediate

GENERAL CARE: Relatively easy to grow, they require moist but not wet soil that has higher than average acidity. Because of this, you will want to amend with something like coffee grounds.

TOXIC: no

VIBRATIONAL KEYWORDS: energy, excitement

TEMPERAMENT: projective

ELEMENT: fire

PLANET: Sun, Mars

ZODIAC: Aries, Leo

MINERAL: fire agate, sunstone, moldavite, carnelian, dravite

TAROT: The Sun

AFFIRMATION: I'm here; this is my time!

MAGICAL EMPLOYMENT: It should be of no surprise that coffee is a great plant to work with when you want to add energy and excitement to something. Growing it in the bedroom brings an increase of sexual activity. Growing it in the kitchen encourages an influx of new recipes and styles. Wherever you grow it, a heightened energy is sure to follow.

Dieffenbachia

Dieffenbachia is a popular houseplant that gets a bad reputation because of its dark past. Well, to be fair, it isn't dieffenbachia that is to blame; rather, it's malicious humans who exploited dieffenbachia's baneful properties to abuse slaves in the Caribbean in the eighteenth century. It is high in a chemical compound called calcium oxalate, which causes irritation to the throat and GI tract and renders the unlucky person who ate it mute and in severe abdominal pain. I'll let you do your own independent research on the history of this and how it led to a problematic common name for this genus. Just know that this plant has so much more to give than what we took from it during that time. Dieffenbachia has large pointed leaves expressing various shades of green and often splashy variegation. They can grow quite tall in the right conditions and are tolerant of low-light situations.

REGION OF ORIGIN: South American tropics and the Caribbean

GROWTH RATE: fast

HABIT: freely clumping, upright

DIFFICULTY LEVEL: beginner

GENERAL CARE: Dieffenbachia is one of the easiest plants to care for, and its cultivars are highly prized for their potential size. They prefer low to bright indirect light and moist, well-draining soil.

TOXIC: yes

VIBRATIONAL KEYWORDS: protection, illusions, truth

TEMPERAMENT: receptive

ELEMENT: water

PLANET: Moon

ZODIAC: Cancer

MINERAL: moonstone, blue calcite, aquamarine, sodalite, chrysoprase, amethyst

TAROT: The Moon

AFFIRMATION: I see through illusion.

MAGICAL EMPLOYMENT: Dieffenbachia can be worked with to silence enemies, repel the evil eye, and break through illusion or lies to reveal the truth behind them. It is ideal to grow this next to the front door as it will help reveal someone's true nature upon entering your home. Additionally, you can grow this near the computer for the same purposes.

Dracaena

DRAGON PALM

Dracaena is a large genus within the asparagus family of succulent-like shrubs that resemble palms. They look a lot like bamboo and a palm tree had a baby. In fact, the plant commonly sold as lucky bamboo is actually *Dracaena sanderiana*. It is no stretch of the imagination to understand why these plants are commonly confused with palms, but when you get up close, you can both see the differences between the two as well as feel them. One species, *Dracaena draco*, is the famous dragon's blood tree, which produces a red sap when cut that is harvested to make sacred incense.

REGION OF ORIGIN: Africa, southern Asia, Australia

GROWTH RATE: slow

HABIT: succulent shrub

DIFFICULTY LEVEL: easy

GENERAL CARE: It can take a dracaena a very long time to grow; general observations suggest perhaps just a few inches for the first couple years and then perhaps up to a foot a year once it is well established. They enjoy bright indirect light but can handle low light and prefer moist and well-draining soil. Propagate through cutting.

TOXIC: yes

VIBRATIONAL KEYWORDS: persistence, impulsivity, goals, desire

TEMPERAMENT: projective

ELEMENT: air

PLANET: Mercury

ZODIAC: Libra, Aquarius

MINERAL: citrine, yellow calcite, clear quartz, blue lace agate

TAROT: Knight of Swords

AFFIRMATION: Once I have made up my mind, no one can stop me.

MAGICAL EMPLOYMENT: While dracaena might be a slow grower, it has a lot of serious power and can be worked with in magic when you have to go against the status quo or feel like you are being backed into a corner. It lifts us up so we can lift others up, and it teaches us how to share what is on our minds in a constructive way. For those who struggle with impulsivity, this plant can guide you through the process of developing methods of control.

Species and Hybrids of Note

D. sanderiana, also known as lucky bamboo, is a common gift as it is easy to take care of and can be manipulated to grow into interesting shapes. In magic I work with this species to bring luck to my endeavors, especially the ones related to my long-term goals. It also has a tendency to help draw energy downward, so it makes a good ally in meditation and high traffic areas.
CARE LEVEL: beginner

D. fragrans 'Massangeana', also known as the corn plant, does have leaves that resemble a variegated maize plant, but it is not, in fact, maize. This is a great plant to grow when you work in a corporate situation or are trying to climb the corporate ladder as it helps us develop eloquence and get attention from our superiors.
CARE LEVEL: beginner

D. surculosa 'Florida Beauty', also known as 'Gold Dust', has green leaves that are speckled with yellow and stays relatively small at around two feet tall when mature. Work with this dracaena if you are a small business owner as it helps us remain persistent and can be placed near a cash register to encourage sales.
CARE LEVEL: beginner

D. marginata, also known as dragon tree, is not the same as *D. draco,* which produces the resin. *Marginata* is dragon-like in a Dr. Seuss sort of way, in that its trunk resembles scales on a dragon tail ending in a ball of leaves. A popular houseplant, work with the dragon tree to protect what's yours.
CARE LEVEL: beginner

Epipremnum

DEVIL'S IVY, POTHOS

Epipremnum is a climbing genus of plants in the aroid family that is easily misidentified with their cousins *Monstera*, *Rhaphidophora*, and *Scindapsus*. They are vigorous growers that showcase large fenestrated leaves and vines that can mature to as much as ten feet in length. Their ability to grow to such large sizes is dependent on whether or not they can climb a host tree or pole; otherwise, they remain in their juvenile form perpetually. There are fifteen recognized species in this genus, with hundreds of cultivars. The two species we are most likely to run into are *E. aureum* (also known as pothos or devil's ivy) and *E. pinnatum*. While *E. pinnatum* is not technically a pothos, it is often referred to as one by sellers, likely due to the market's familiarity with *E. aureum*.

REGION OF ORIGIN: Asia, the Pacific Islands, Australia

GROWTH RATE: fast

HABIT: climbing/vining

DIFFICULTY LEVEL: beginner to intermediate

GENERAL CARE: They prefer well-draining soil that is allowed to dry out a little between each watering. They also require something to climb on if you want their leaves to gain size; otherwise, they do

wonderfully as a hanging basket, are low-light tolerant, and make great beginner plants. Most cultivars are easy to take care of and can be propagated through leaf cutting.

TOXIC: yes

VIBRATIONAL KEYWORDS: strategy, problem solving, manifestation, determination

TEMPERAMENT: projective

ELEMENT: fire

PLANET: Jupiter, Mars

ZODIAC: Sagittarius, Aries

MINERAL: peridot, moldavite, green kyanite, clear quartz, labradorite

TAROT: Queen of Wands

AFFIRMATION: I bring joy to the tasks that challenge me.

MAGICAL EMPLOYMENT: Epipremnum grow incredibly fast when given the chance and bring with them a very fiery energy that can be seen in their leaves after they begin to mature, with each looking like a green flame suspended from a vine. I work with them when I need assistance moving through blocks and obstacles or when I feel stuck or confused, and to help me manifest dreams into reality once their leaves are mature. They are very easy to care for and can be grown anywhere to help keep energy moving and encourage other plants to grow.

Species and Hybrids of Note

E. aureum is the original plant from which there are now well over twenty cultivars that come and go from the market. This includes *E. aureum* 'Marble Queen', *E. aureum* 'Neon', *E. aureum* 'Jessenia', *E. aureum* 'Manjula', and so on. Each has a different variegation pattern that plays on a palette of dark green to pure white. They are all beautiful, but energetically they all feel the same to me and are great to work with in scrying. Check out the options available and see which one feels the best in your home or do what I did and go on a collecting spree and treat them like they are Pokémon!

E. pinnatum comes in a handful of cultivars, most notably *E. pinnatum* 'Cebu Blue' and *E. pinnatum variegata.* Again, I wish I had more to report here, but they feel oriented toward the same ends as all other epipremnum.

Fern

POLYPODIOPHYTA

Ferns have been around for over three hundred and sixty million years and can be found all over the planet, especially in places where flowering plants tend to struggle to survive for one reason or another. There are almost eleven thousand species within this class, though most of those aren't suitable for the average home environment. They reproduce via spores, and each leaf contains a complex network of veins that leads back to the stem (frond). In general, ferns prefer moist, humid conditions; however, some have adapted to grow epiphytically with little water. Ferns are one of the few houseplants that have a longstanding magical association, and growing them can be a fun way of tuning into some of that old-world magic.

REGION OF ORIGIN: globally, excluding those regions with arctic conditions

GROWTH RATE: slow

HABIT: clumping

DIFFICULTY LEVEL: intermediate

GENERAL CARE: Ferns can be difficult in the home if you have low humidity and should be placed in well-draining, loamy soil unless otherwise noted. Water frequently and mist often.

TOXIC: some are

VIBRATIONAL KEYWORDS: love, grace, beauty, adoration, psychic insight

TEMPERAMENT: projective

ELEMENT: water

PLANET: Pluto, Venus

ZODIAC: Pisces

MINERAL: chrysoprase, chlorite, moldavite, spirit quartz, jade

TAROT: Ten of Cups

AFFIRMATION: I am worth loving completely.

MAGICAL EMPLOYMENT: Ferns are classically associated with love and are often worked with in love spells. I want to take that a step further and extend their influence to include beauty and grace because it isn't just love that they promote, but adoration. They bring about a majestic quality to beauty and glamour workings and aid their growers with enhanced intuition and psychic insight. They should be grown near the altar or meditation space to assist in communication with the underworld and near the bed to bring about prophetic dreams.

Species and Hybrids of Note

There is no way to cover the entire fern group, but I think there are a handful of ferns that should make an appearance in your home.

Adiantum, also known as the maidenhair fern, is a wispy-leaved fern with small, thin leaves that is often described as dainty. This is a great fern to work with when you want a lover to be more considerate of your needs.
CARE LEVEL: intermediate

Nephrolepis exaltata, also known as the Boston fern, is a bushy variety with feathery leaves that is easy to care for and grows vigorously. I work with it as a type of psychic satellite for my extrasensory perception (ESP), allowing me to extend the reach of my psychic field.
CARE LEVEL: intermediate

Platycerium bifurcatum, also known as the staghorn fern, is a broad-leafed fern with flat, silvery foliage that tends to separate into fingerlike structures. Work with this fern when you want to dominate energies in the bedroom and attract romantic partners.
CARE LEVEL: intermediate

Phlebodium aureum, also known as the rabbit's foot fern, is a smaller foliage variety that produces fuzzy fronds that extend from the rhizome, resembling the paws of some woodland creature. These are excellent partners in magic that is related to attracting compassionate, romantic partners as well as softening the language used between partners.
CARE LEVEL: intermediate

Asplenium nidus, the bird's nest fern, is a broad-leaf variety that can grow to large sizes. Its leaves respond to light quality and will ruffle when exposed to brighter light. It is a great ally in love magic for attracting a long-term partner.

CARE LEVEL: intermediate

Ficus

MORACEAE FAMILY

Ficus are collectively known as figs or fig trees. There are around eight hundred and fifty species in this family, and they range from vining plants to large, stately trees. Growing in the jungle, fig trees tend to be extremely important food sources for several species of wildlife. In 2006 archeologists found remains of the common fig, *F. carica*, near a village close to the ancient city of Jericho, suggesting that it was the first crop intentionally grown in the Middle East, predating wheat by nearly a thousand years. The common fig is mentioned in the Christian Bible and remains a widely cultivated fruit in the Middle East and Mediterranean. The bodhi tree (*F. religiosa*) is said to be the tree that the Buddha was sitting under when he received enlightenment. In Hinduism *F. religiosa* is also known as *aśvattha*, a concept parallel to the world tree of Indo-European mythology. Some ficus can live thousands of years and reach heights of well over one hundred feet tall.

REGION OF ORIGIN: tropical Africa and Asia, Mediterranean

GROWTH RATE: moderate

HABIT: tree, vining, shrub

DIFFICULTY LEVEL: beginner to advanced

GENERAL CARE: Ficus have a range of needs, so it is best to research your specific species. In general, an all-purpose potting mix will work well. They prefer bright indirect light. Some species do not handle fluctuations in humidity or moisture well; others prefer to dry out before watering. Propagate through stem cutting.

TOXIC: Only the fruit is nontoxic. This is a latex-producing plant, so avoid skin contact with the liquid.

VIBRATIONAL KEYWORDS: wisdom, sanctity, sacredness, spiritual awareness, gnosis

TEMPERAMENT: projective

ELEMENT: earth

PLANET: Venus

ZODIAC: Taurus

MINERAL: leopardite, sandstone, jade, prehnite, hematite, clear quartz

TAROT: The Wheel of Fortune

AFFIRMATION: I am one with all that is around me.

MAGICAL EMPLOYMENT: Ficus are awesome energy to have around if you are someone who considers themselves to be on a spiritual journey or are seeking to understand how your life fits into the grand scheme of things. They are teachers of spiritual knowledge that guide us through the realms of mind, body, and spirit. They help us find our calling and remain steadfast while on our path. They are allies in meditation especially and help us develop practices in our spiritual life that lead to deep understanding of the universe and the cultivation of meaningful gnosis.

Species and Hybrids of Note

There are a lot of potential ficus housemates that could make a great fit in your spiritual practice. Here are some of the most popular on the market and a little about their unique spiritual properties.

F. lyrata, also known as the fiddle-leaf fig, produces large, thick, broad leaves and can grow quite large. They make excellent partners when developing spiritual talents related to communication with the dead.

CARE LEVEL: advanced

F. elastica, or the rubber tree, has large, glossy, oval leaves that are thick and deeply colored. There are a few cultivars; the *F. elastica* 'Ruby' is a burgundy variety, and there are variegated versions of both the standard and ruby varieties. These trees are great to partner with when seeking answers about your past and ancestral connections; they also assist in communication with spirits.

CARE LEVEL: intermediate

F. benjamina, also known as the weeping fig, is probably the most common ficus on the houseplant market. Its small leaves help make this plant look like a miniature tree. It is an incredible ally for those of us who travel on the astral plane as it helps us find our way to and back from our destination with ease.

CARE LEVEL: beginner

F. benghalensis, also known as banyan or Ficus Audrey, is a faster-growing species that can reach great heights when given the right conditions. This ficus in particular is the one I work with when accessing the Akashic records.

CARE LEVEL: advanced

F. religiosa is actually not that difficult to raise indoors; however, with time it will grow to great height, so keeping it trimmed is a must. I have mentioned its religious importance to both Buddhists and Hindus, and I can say that there is something special about this particular ficus. It does feel holy, and it does instantly connect us to the world tree, similar to how the oak tree does. Working with this plant in your practice will help you travel in your dreams, receive wisdom during meditation, and help you understand your divine purpose.

CARE LEVEL: advanced

Gesneriad Family

GESNERIACEAE

The gesneriad family is home to some of the most beloved species within the houseplant hobby. They include classic plants like the African violet (*Saintpaulia*), lipstick plant (*Aeschynanthus*), Cape primrose (*Streptocarpus*), and others, which are each widely in cultivation. They are generally easy to care for, with some being woody and others more herbaceous, and they can be found in a wide range of environments. They are usually divided into two subfamilies, the Old World (*Didymocarpoideae*) and New World (*Gesnerioideae*). One major difference between the two seems to be that new-world gesneriads have flowers adapted for pollination from hummingbirds whereas old-world species tend to have a wide range of pollination tactics.

REGION OF ORIGIN: subtropical and tropical regions throughout the world

GROWTH RATE: intermediate

HABIT: trailing shrub or herbaceous

DIFFICULTY LEVEL: moderate

GENERAL CARE: Preferring temperatures between 65 and 80°F, gesneriads do well in bright indirect light and in a well-draining all-purpose potting mix. Some species require humidity between 50 and 70 percent.

TOXIC: The majority of species are nontoxic.

VIBRATIONAL KEYWORDS: peace, unconditional love, divine feminine, forgiveness

TEMPERAMENT: passive

ELEMENT: water, earth

PLANET: Venus

ZODIAC: Taurus, Libra

MINERAL: rhodonite, amazonite, rose quartz, morganite, merlinite, blue calcite

TAROT: Queen of Cups

AFFIRMATION: The love I have for others brings me peace.

MAGICAL EMPLOYMENT: Gesneriads are a diverse bunch, but throughout the genera there seems to be an absolute connection to the forces of the divine feminine, and I recommend growing them as an act of devotion to these forces. I have also noticed that people who are attracted to these plants also have a propensity toward enjoying creating green spaces as a form of sanctuary and meditative practice. Gesneriads facilitate the cultivation of gnosis and help us connect to the spark of divine love inside each of us, making them great allies for those who struggle with solitude.

Species and Hybrids of Note

Within the gesneriad family there are three thousand five hundred species and an uncountable number of cultivars. While not all of them are suited for every home environment, there are a couple that have become stars for their ease of care, and I think that warrants giving them a shout-out.

Aeschynanthus, also known as the lipstick plant, is a succulent-like gesneriad with green and sometimes black variegated leaves. It should be worked with for magic related to embracing the power of the divine feminine within and bringing that energy outward into the world.

CARE LEVEL: beginner

Nematanthus, or the goldfish plant, produces flowers that resemble tiny goldfish. It is particularly well-suited to bringing peace and stability to areas of the home where people gather.

CARE LEVEL: beginner

Saintpaulia, otherwise known as the African violet, is a herbaceous gesneriad that is not at all closely related to the actual violet. *Fun fact:* African violets have a unique trait in that they respond to radiation by changes in growth. Depending on the method, this can change flower color, add variegation to leaves, and even alter the growth rate. Several cultivars have been created this way. Work with them as meditation partners and to help create a sense of sanctuary and peace within your home.

CARE LEVEL: beginner

Episcia cupreata, also known as the flame violet, is also not a true violet, though it has arguably the most colorful foliage within the gesneriad family. Some cultivars and species produce purple and silver leaves with bright red flowers. They do require moderate to high humidity. Grow these when you want to forgive yourself or others for things that happened in the past so you can move on. CARE LEVEL: intermediate

Streptocarpus, also known as the Cape primrose, is a herbaceous variety that has fuzzy foliage and develops large flowers that bloom in the spring and range in color. They are a fantastic addition to your collection, especially if you are looking for a splash of color. Grow these to work with the energies of unconditional love. CARE LEVEL: beginner

Hoya Family

WAX PLANTS

The *Hoya* genus, commonly called wax plants, is made up of mostly woody epiphytic evergreens with succulent-type leaves. Foliage ranges in shape and presentation; some leaves are small and needlelike, others large and furry, but most are smooth and glossy, often looking waxed. They are trailing plants that can grow anywhere from three to sixty feet in length. They perform well in hanging baskets but prefer to be trellised.

What makes the hoya especially interesting—and, in my opinion, magical—is its inflorescence, which produces as a cluster of flowers at the end of a modified piece of stem called a pendunclе. First of all, "penduncle" is fun to say, and I think we should all appreciate it. Second, and more importantly, is that these flowers produce amazing scents that often seem synthetic. For example, the *H. carnosa* has a flower that is scented like chocolate; *H.* 'Christine' smells of lemon; *H. imperialis* smells like rose, and *H. bilobata* smells like vanilla caramel. There are some hoya that produce flowers with unpleasant scents as well, such as *H. coronaria,* which smells of burning rubber; *H. elliptica,* which is said to resemble yeasty dough; and *H. pubicorolla* ssp. *anthracina,* which is purported to reek of smoked ham.

REGION OF ORIGIN: throughout Asia and part of Australia

GROWTH RATE: moderate

HABIT: trailing, succulent-like, epiphytic

DIFFICULTY LEVEL: beginner to advanced

GENERAL CARE: Hoyas thrive in chunky, well-draining substrate and are highly vulnerable to root rot, so they should never be left in standing water. They prefer higher humidity but can do quite well in low humidity, depending on the species. Propagate through cutting. Hoyas make excellent terrarium plants. They tend to be mostly pest free but are like candy to mealy bugs.

TOXIC: no

VIBRATIONAL KEYWORDS: excitement, communication, inspiration, planning, attention

TEMPERAMENT: projective

ELEMENT: air

PLANET: Mercury

ZODIAC: Gemini, Aquarius

MINERAL: hiddenite, Herkimer diamond, citrine, fluorite, topaz, apatite

TAROT: Page of Swords

AFFIRMATION: My excitement fuels my day.

MAGICAL EMPLOYMENT: Hoyas are a very fun family to work with in magic because they tend to bring a lot of excitement to every project they are invited to be part of. You can make a flower essence with their flowers that can be added to teas or a ritual bath. Hoyas are one of the first plants I turn to when seeking inspiration or help with writer's block. They are great magical partners for anyone who works in communications, publishing, or content creation as they help to generate new ideas and can help attract new followers.

Species and Hybrids of Note

There are over five hundred species of hoya and an untold number of cultivars. Most of these never make it onto the plant market because of their care needs, but a handful circulate plant stores quite regularly. Here are five hoyas that I recommend buying if you come across them.

H. pubicalyx is a fast-growing variety with several hybrids whose flowers range from black to pale pink. Their flowers smell woody to floral, and in magic they are excellent problem solvers. Work with them when you need to strategize, especially regarding career.

CARE LEVEL: beginner

H. carnosa is another fast grower with what is likely hundreds of hybrids. Its flowers often smell of chocolate or warm sugar. In magic I often turn to this when I want the attention of others and include it in love workings.

CARE LEVEL: beginner

H. kentiana has thin, pointy leaves that fade from dark red to green as they mature and produce a red flower that smells of butterscotch. This species is fantastic to work with when you want to attract business partners, and it facilitates communication between groups.

CARE LEVEL: beginner

H. australis is easy to care for and can grow fast. It has broad pointed leaves with flowers that are scented like hyacinth with a hint of musk. They are great companions in magic related to dreams and dream interpretation.

CARE LEVEL: beginner

H. multiflora has thin dark green leaves and produces clusters of white and yellow flowers that look like shooting stars and are scented like freshly cut herbs. Work with this plant to receive divine inspiration and work with spirit guides.

CARE LEVEL: intermediate

Marantaceae Family

PRAYER PLANTS

Calathea, *Maranta*, and *Stromanthe* are genera of the family Marantaceae and have very similar characteristics. They are so similar that they get confused for one another often. They each have cultivars with beautiful colors with a similar shape and growth habit. The difference between them is that marantas have bold striped patterns, come in a variety of leaf shapes, and undergo a process called "nyctinasty" where the leaves fold upward at night, giving them the common name of prayer plant. Stromanthe also undergo nyctinasty; however, they require constant tropical conditions to thrive and therefore don't often make it onto the market.

Calathea usually have round, thicker leaves that can display a wide range of colors, from black to an almost neon pink. Even though they don't undergo nyctinasty like the marantas, they are still often referred to as prayer plants due to the shared similarities; they are also often called peacock plants. In 2012 a large subgroup of calathea were reclassified as belonging to the genus *Goeppertia* after genetic tests confirmed that they had separate ancestral heritage. However, because they are so similar and are often sold as calathea, I have chosen to include them with calathea.

REGION OF ORIGIN: South America

GROWTH RATE: moderate

HABIT: spreading

DIFFICULTY LEVEL: intermediate

GENERAL CARE: Marantaceae are known for being drama queens, so much so that the "plant internet" is full of memes created by bemoaning owners. They drop leaves and brown at the edges when their needs aren't being met or at the first sign of trouble. They prefer moderately moist soil, higher humidity, and moderate to bright indirect light. They do not handle regular tap water well; use rain, distilled, or fish tank water. Propagate through division.

TOXIC: no

VIBRATIONAL KEYWORDS: deities, psychic sensitivity, spirituality, spirit guides

TEMPERAMENT: receptive

ELEMENT: water

PLANET: Pluto

ZODIAC: Scorpio

MINERAL: amethyst, opal, tourmaline, calcite, aquamarine, angelite

TAROT: Judgement, Death

AFFIRMATION: My spirit is connected to all.

MAGICAL EMPLOYMENT: Working with the Marantaceae family in general connects to a cultivated sense of spirituality in a way that not all plants can. It brings us in alignment with the natural flow of spirit that pours through our lives and can afford us the ability to perceive the otherwise imperceivable. As an aid in magic, they are especially great for spirit communication, including the dead, and should be raised near ancestral altars and shrines if possible. What I find most fascinating about these plants is their propensity to assist in processing psychic and spiritual information.

Species and Hybrids of Note

There is a wide range of plants in the Marantaceae family, but the following are some of my favorite to work with in magic.

CALATHEAS (and *Goeppertias*) can be tricky to grow, but once you figure them out, they are quite enjoyable plants to partner with in magic. There are over sixty species within this genus, and several hybrids have been created. These are a few that stick out.

G. orbifolia has large circular silver-striped leaves and is easily found, even in hardware stores. It is a great partner in helping us connect with ghosts and residual psychic energy.
CARE LEVEL: intermediate

G. roseopicta is one of the most popular species for indoor use and has impressive painted foliage, with four shades of green on top and a burgundy red underside. There are several hybrids of this species available. I work with these when I want to connect with spirits related to gardening and hortocculture, such as green guides and fairies.
CARE LEVEL: intermediate

G. kegeljanii, also known as *Calathea* 'Musaica' and *Calathea* 'Network', has long oval two-tone leaves that express a very unique, almost reticulated patterning that does indeed give off matrix vibes. I work with this one to help me better partner with the spirits of technology and the internet.
CARE LEVEL: intermediate

G. insignis, also known as *Calathea lancifolia* and the rattlesnake plant, is a long leafed variety with a two-tone painted leaf and a burgundy underside. It is a particularly great ally in work related to the Muses and creativity.
CARE LEVEL: intermediate

MARANTAS seem particularly equipped to handle relationships with divine beings. While they are intermediate to advanced, those with the confidence to explore a relationship with them will find their sensitivity is a form of communication.

M. leuconeura is the mother species to what is believed to be hundreds of cultivars, and its name means "white vein." I find these plants to be particularly in tune with the divine feminine.
CARE LEVEL: intermediate to advanced

M. bicolor is highly popular, with its two-tone leaves that look as though they were dabbed with a paintbrush. This variety is great at helping us connect with spirits of place and build partnerships with them.
CARE LEVEL: intermediate

STROMANTHE are the rarest finds in the Maranta family as they typically don't do well in drier settings. The most common is the *S. sanguinea*, which is a bit more tolerant of household conditions. Of its cultivars, one sticks out.

S. sanguinea 'Triostar' is the most popular and one that I often turn to for work related to communicating with my ancestors as its patterns alternate and I use them to divine simple yes and no questions.
CARE LEVEL: advanced

Medinilla

ROSE GRAPE

For those seeking something a little different than the usual big leaves or trailing vines, *Medinilla magnifica* may have what you are looking for. With relatively plain leaves, the medinilla relies on its unique inflorescence to showcase its stunning beauty. A specialized stem emerges from its foliage that produces clusters of pink, purple, red, white, or yellow flowers that hang down like grapes. It is sometimes referred to as the Malaysian orchid, though it is not a member of the orchid family. Their size (mature specimens can grow to four feet tall) and their abundant flowers make them a fantastic addition to your indoor plant collection.

REGION OF ORIGIN: Asia, Pacific Islands, Madagascar

GROWTH RATE: moderate

HABIT: shrub

DIFFICULTY LEVEL: intermediate to advanced

GENERAL CARE: Well-draining but moist soil with indirect bright light and temperatures that stay between 55 and 80°F. Remove dead flowers to promote new growth. Blooms in spring through summer. Propagate by cutting or seed.

TOXIC: no

VIBRATIONAL KEYWORDS: girlboss, divine feminine, entrepreneurship, business

TEMPERAMENT: projective

ELEMENT: earth

PLANET: Venus

ZODIAC: Capricorn, Taurus, Virgo

MINERAL: dalmatian jasper, amazonite, pyrite, moss agate, malachite, amber

TAROT: Ace of Wands

AFFIRMATION: Business comes to me, and I am prepared for it.

MAGICAL EMPLOYMENT: Medinilla is another plant that feels deeply connected to the divine feminine, and this becomes more evident as it grows and produces more flowering clusters. It also has a business-oriented energy that responds well to entrepreneurs and business owners, especially those who embrace and work with the divine feminine. Because of this, I loving refer to it as the girlboss plant. Excellent for long-term planning, attracting customers and clients, and rising to the top of your game.

Monstera Genus

SWISS CHEESE PLANTS

The *Monstera* genus is home to one of the most popular houseplants on the planet: the *Monstera deliciosa.* Monsteras are famous for their large sizes as well as the holes and fenestrations that their leaves produce as they mature. It is speculated that the holes serve to allow wind to pass through the leaves without damaging them; others suggest that it could be an adaptation to regulate temperature or possibly even for the purposes of light distribution. Whatever the reason, this genus is generally easy to care for and fast growing. In the wild they use aerial roots to latch onto trees and then use their vine to climb up the tree as high as seventy feet.

REGION OF ORIGIN: tropical South America

GROWTH RATE: fast

HABIT: climbing

DIFFICULTY LEVEL: beginner to advanced

GENERAL CARE: Prefer chunky, well-draining soil that is allowed to dry out a little between waterings. Most species are great with temperatures above 50°F; some, however, require heavy amounts of humidity.

TOXIC: yes

VIBRATIONAL KEYWORDS: protection, determination, strength, expansion, collaboration

TEMPERAMENT: projective

ELEMENT: fire, water

PLANET: Pluto, Jupiter

ZODIAC: Sagittarius, Pisces, Scorpio

MINERAL: clear quartz, rose quartz, obsidian, moonstone, lepidolite

TAROT: The Hierophant

AFFIRMATION: I am strong, and my influence is expansive.

MAGICAL EMPLOYMENT: All monsteras are vigorous growers and love to bring that energy to whatever work we do with them. I know you might be looking at the list of correspondences here and thinking that I have gone a little mad, but the truth is that some species have a uniquely underworld quality to them, while the entire genus can produce leaves that look like flames. Monsteras are protective and fierce, but some of them feel steeped in energies that are quite the opposite. Let's take a look at five monsteras that make great magical companions.

Species and Hybrids of Note

M. deliciosa, also called the Swiss cheese plant, has large fenestrated leaves that can grow to around thirty-five inches in length and diameter. They are fiercely protective of their caregivers and, if given everything they need to thrive, will help get other plants in the immediate area to cooperate with one another on magical projects. Variegated varieties of the *deliciosa* are available at a much more expensive price; these make great allies when developing healthy new relationships with people.

CARE LEVEL: beginner

M. adansonii, sometimes called Swiss cheese vine, is another popular houseplant that has large pointed leaves with holes. This particular monstera makes a good hanging basket addition to the home and is poised to bring perseverance and determination to your magic.

CARE LEVEL: beginner

M. epipremnoides, also known as *Monstera esqueleto,* is similar to *adansonii* but much larger and the holes are much wider, giving the leaves a skeletal look. They are great to work with when seeking the protection of your ancestors, communicating with the dead, and seeking advice from deities.

CARE LEVEL: intermediate

M. siltepecana has silver coloring and veining while immature, but as it is allowed to mature it loses this luster and eventually takes on a deep green with large oblong holes. It can be kept small by growing in a hanging basket and allowing to vine. Work with it in magic to protect investments, businesses, and loved ones.
CARE LEVEL: intermediate

M. dubia is a shingling variety that starts off with small silvery leaves that attach themselves to bark or siding and then slowly mature to form large fenestrated leaves that resemble flames. Work with this species to communicate with faery beings and for secrecy.
CARE LEVEL: intermediate

Orchid Family

ORCHIDACEAE

The orchid family makes up around 11 percent of seed-producing plants on the planet and has over twenty-eight thousand species, with an untold number of hybrids and cultivars. They are primarily epiphytic and have adapted to live in almost every region of the planet that isn't covered in ice for most of the year. Being such a diverse and resilient family, altogether they make up the second-largest family of flowering plant on the planet, and chances are you have local varieties that are being sold near you that will do excellent in your home. Otherwise, there are plenty in circulation to choose from.

REGION OF ORIGIN: every non-glacial region

GROWTH RATE: slow to moderate

HABIT: epiphytic bulb

DIFFICULTY LEVEL: beginner to advanced

GENERAL CARE: Orchids prefer a bark-filled, chunky substrate that allows for plenty of air to circulate around their thick roots, which are capable of photosynthesis. Most orchids prefer bright indirect light and humidity. See your species for propagation advice.

TOXIC: Most are nontoxic and pet friendly.

VIBRATIONAL KEYWORDS: love, sensuality, romance, seduction

TEMPERAMENT: projective

ELEMENT: fire

PLANET: Jupiter

ZODIAC: Sagittarius

MINERAL: rose quartz, morganite, aquamarine, emerald, ruby, fire agate, topaz

TAROT: Two of Cups

AFFIRMATION: I attract healthy sexual partners.

MAGICAL EMPLOYMENT: In flower folklore orchids are generally associated with the upper class and being refined; they are thought to bring an air of civility to their location. In modern times we work them into wedding ceremonies, corsages for dances, and find them generally around the big moments that define us a romantic and sexual people. Orchid scent in perfumes is also used in folk magic for seduction. While there is absolutely an energy of elegance and finery, there is also an energy that is quite sensual and sexy to them. Even their name is derived from a word that means "testicle."

Genera of Note

Cattleya are also known as corsage orchids as well as queen orchids and are one of the most popular among the family, with over fifty species within the genus. They are divided into two groups, the first being unifoliate, with one large leaf and large flower per stem, and the second being bifoliate, which have two leaves per stem and multiple small flowers. They are among some of the most fragrant in the orchid kingdom and are relatively easy to care for. Work with cattleya in your magic to increase self-confidence and help heal from past abusive romantic relationships. Cattleya are especially good for helping us find innocent excitement in our love lives. CARE LEVEL: beginner to intermediate

Cymbidium, sometimes referred to as boat orchids, is a genus prized for its decorative flower spike (inflorescence) that generally has a triple-lobed lip. They come in a range of colors and sizes and are lightly scented. These are great to work with in magic focused on self-love and appreciation, and I highly recommend them to people who are going through a breakup, as they ease the transition and recenter it around healing and moving forward. CARE LEVEL: beginner to intermediate

Phalaenopsis orchids, also known as moth orchids, are the ones most frequently seen in home goods stores and supermarkets. They are hardier than many orchids and produce large inflorescence with large, colorful flowers. Most species produce flowers that can last up to four months; however, they are not particularly fragrant.

Work with these to attract sexual partnerships and experiences that are healthy and affirming. Excellent for those who are dating.
CARE LEVEL: beginner to intermediate

Paphiopedilum are probably my personal favorite orchid to partner with in magic. Often referred to as slipper orchids, this genus has plain to spotted leaves with multicolored flowers that have a distinctive floral pouch. The flowers are often spotted and striped, giving off a wild jungle vibe—which makes sense as they are jungle orchids! They have one flower that develops on the end of a stem. They are adaptable and make excellent beginner orchids for the witch who wants something that will help add a little bit of spice to the bedroom. They can also be worked with to improve the romantic life of an existing partnership. Sleeping with them next to the bed can conjure dreams from Faery.
CARE LEVEL: beginner

Vanilla is a spice orchid whose flowers produce the famous bean that we use for that lovely flavor. You won't find this in your local hardware store, but you can find them online from growers at reasonable prices. They vine and do require time and patience. In-home pollination can easily be done during a small window of time and can lead to pods that are extra potent in magic because you grew them yourself. Especially good for love and seduction magic, these orchids require special conditions such as higher humidity but can bring a whole new potency to your love magic.
CARE LEVEL: intermediate to advanced

Peperomia

RADIATOR PLANTS

Peperomia are generally smaller houseplants that reach up to around a foot tall. They are known for their colorful succulent-like foliage and ease of care. The name "radiator plant" comes from the fact that many do well in bright, dry environments such as those in a windowsill above a radiator. While this is true, there are still plenty of species who evolved in cloud forests and prefer higher humidity levels if they are to thrive; such is the case for the highly popular *P. caperata.* They are members of the pepper family, and some varieties are used in both cooking and medicine, though it is not advised to eat your houseplants as some species might be mildly toxic.

REGION OF ORIGIN: tropical and subtropical regions globally

GROWTH RATE: moderate

HABIT: clumping and rhizomatous

DIFFICULTY LEVEL: beginner to intermediate

GENERAL CARE: In general, a well-draining soil that is allowed to dry about 50 percent before thoroughly watering is ideal. Most prefer bright indirect to moderate direct sunlight depending on the species. As a group, peperomia are highly suspectable to root rot.

TOXIC: Most are nontoxic.

VIBRATIONAL KEYWORDS: community and shared connections

TEMPERAMENT: receptive

ELEMENT: water

PLANET: Moon

ZODIAC: Cancer, Scorpio, Pisces

MINERAL: amethyst, pearl, goldstone, celestite, aventurine, clear quartz

TAROT: The High Priestess

AFFIRMATION: My psychic senses are clear and insightful.

MAGICAL EMPLOYMENT: There is something special about peperomias, and I have enjoyed collecting them to add to my magic. They tend to work well with one another; whereas in some cases having multiple varieties of the same plant can make the energies feel competitive, peperomia very much enjoys the teamwork. They are very spiritual and psychic plants whose tenderness and succulent nature speak to their kindness. They are great partners in magic for those of us who are psychic as they help to increase extrasensory perception and channeling. Grow them near the altar to aid in magical processes or near the bed to increase psychic dreaming. Peperomias coax people's magical abilities to emerge, making them great meditative allies.

Species and Hybrids of Note

There are several peperomia out on the market, but if I had just three that I could recommend having in your collection, these would be them.

P. caperata has small, wrinkled, deep emerald foliage with reddish brown stems. It is the mother plant to several cultivars such as the 'Chameleon,' 'Ruby,' and 'Painted Lady.' They are fantastic little allies who enhance clairvoyance and clairaudience, and placing them where you perform psychic readings can help boost clarity in your sessions.
CARE LEVEL: beginner

P. polybotrya, also known as the owl eye peperomia, has emerald teardrop-shaped leaves and is one of a handful of peperomia that can easily size up to fifteen inches, with the leaves increasingly getting wider. This is similar and closely related to *Pilea peperomioides,* which is not a peperomia but looks almost identical to this species and has similar magical properties. They are great helpers when communicating with spirit guides, teachers, and other spirit allies as they enhance mediumship.
CARE LEVEL: intermediate

P. argyreia has large teardrop-shaped leaves with silver striping and is commonly known as watermelon peperomia. It is an especially good partner in magic related to spirits that are higher in vibration such as spirit guides, angels, and ancestors.
CARE LEVEL: beginner

Philodendron

GENUS

The genus *Philodendron* is still very much a mystery to the botanical community, with species being added or removed on a semi-regular basis as new discoveries are made. As a result, there are several species that were introduced to the plant community as a philodendron and remain grouped to them even after they end up being rearranged into another genus. This was the case with the popular *Philodendron selloum*, which was reclassified as a *Thaumatophyllum* in 2018. That being said, *Philodendron* is a huge genus of over five hundred species that, for the most part, tend to be well-suited for indoor life.

Their name means "love tree" in Latin as the leaves of all philodendron classically resemble the shape of a heart, and most species climb up trees using a vining stalk and aerial roots. Philodendrons tend to account for some of the least expensive and most expensive plants on the market, depending on the species or cultivar. Many houseplant enthusiasts collect philodendron species for their diverse foliage options and ease of care. The easiest way to divide the philodendron we are likely to grow in our homes is by their most basic growth habits: crawling, climbing, and upright (or self-heading).

REGION OF ORIGIN: South America

GROWTH RATE: fast

HABIT: climbing, upright

DIFFICULTY LEVEL: beginner to advanced

GENERAL CARE: Philodendrons prefer bright indirect light, well-draining soil, and higher humidity, though many species can handle normal household humidity levels. Some do well in hanging baskets, some are upright self-stabilizing types; however, they all benefit from having a pole or something to climb on if you wish to increase leaf size.

TOXIC: yes

VIBRATIONAL KEYWORDS: love, passion, determination, focus, strategy

TEMPERAMENT: projective and receptive, depending on species

ELEMENT: fire, water

PLANET: Jupiter, Neptune, Moon

ZODIAC: Sagittarius, Pisces, Cancer

MINERAL: amethyst, moonstone, carnelian, labradorite, clear quartz, serpentine

TAROT: The Chariot

AFFIRMATION: My will is strong enough to move mountains.

MAGICAL EMPLOYMENT: *Philodendron* is another multi-frequency genus of plant, with variations on a theme throughout each species. In general, as their name suggests, their magic is centered around love—not mushy, romantic love or self-love but a universal love that exceeds limitations. From this love a fire emerges that is capable of sculpting and shaping reality. This love is as sovereign and majestic as it is fierce and determined. It is closer to the love a king or queen might have for their kingdom and its citizens. Different aspects of this personality make themselves known with each species. In general, work with them when you are expanding your empire, making your way to bigger and better places in life, and developing both emotional and mental maturity.

Species and Hybrids of Note

Let's take a look at how we can partner with different philos based on their growth habits.

CRAWLING PHILODENDRON, also known as creeping philodendron, have a thick vine stalk that crawls along the top of the soil. They send petioles up into the air and form leaves that resemble those of an alocasia. They aren't drawn to climb like other philos, instead spending their lives happily on the jungle floor. These bring the classic energy of love with them in a warm and fuzzy kind of way. They are very posh plants and are excellent for those who wish to bring in Cancerian energies.

P. gloriosum has silver veining and soft, velvety leaves that are a light pink when they emerge but fade to a dark, dusty green. Excellent for magic related to the home and hearth as well as service and devotion. A similar species, *P. mamei,* has silver variegation and feels energetically identical with the addition of protection.
CARE LEVEL: beginner

P. pastazanum looks like a gloriosum on steroids, growing to quite large sizes. It is excellent for magic related to the family and should be grown in high-traffic areas around the home. A similar species, *P. plowmanii*, lacks the silver veining but does have ruffled leaves. While its energy is complementary to that of the *pastazanum*, it does seem to be better at helping to clear negative energy and feelings within familial ties.
CARE LEVEL: beginner

CLIMBING PHILODENDRON require a tree, trellis, or pole to climb; however, in some cases they can be grown in a hanging basket when you want the plant to trail and the leaves to remain small. A lot of the smaller species of philodendron that we see belong to this category, such as *P. hederaceum* (also known as the heartleaf philodendron) or *P. brandtianum*. It is home to some larger species as well, such as *P. verrucosum* and *P. burle-marxii* (Burle Marx philodendron). These plants feel very Piscean to me. They envelop their space and spread out to be as comfortable as they possibly can. Magically, they bring intuition to the process of planning and empathy to the needs of others. They heighten emotional awareness and bring focus to the creative process. While I would love to list them all, here are a few of my personal favorites.

P. hederaceum 'Brasil' is a heartleaf philodendron with a light green stripe that runs through the center of the leaf. They seem to reach out to bring comfort to us, and I work with them a lot when focusing on emotional healing.
CARE LEVEL: beginner

P. camposportoanum starts off with a heart shape but matures to an interesting shield shape. I work with this philo a lot for emotional protection and confidence.
CARE LEVEL: beginner

P. verrucosum has dark green velvety leaves and furry petioles. It is sensitive to humidity and drying, but it is quite an exquisite species. Work with it when you want to increase emotional communication and understanding in the home. You can also work with it to gain emotional understanding at work or school.
CARE LEVEL: intermediate

P. micans is a velvety, heart-shaped leaf that we typically grow to remain small and allow to trail. It is particularly good with magic related to intuition and can be grown near the bed to help bring prophetic dreams.
CARE LEVEL: beginner

UPRIGHT PHILODENDRON, also called self-heading philodendron, don't require a support to grow but do benefit from one, allowing them to maximize their leaf size. Generally speaking, these philodendrons have large sagittate leaves that vary in design and color. Their shape and size give them Sagittarius vibes, and I work a lot with them in matters of expansion, planning, and education. There are quite a few, but here is a handful of my favorites.

P. erubescens is the parent plant to several cultivars and hybrids on the market, some of which make up a group that is sometimes referred to as the "royal philodendrons" such as the 'Pink Princess', 'White Wizard', and the 'Royal Queen.' Other well-known cultivars include 'McColley's Finale', 'Painted Lady', and 'Black Cardinal', among others. Work with these in magic for success, triumph, and protection of your assets.

CARE LEVEL: beginner

P. tatei, also known as 'Congo Rojo' or 'Congo', is very similar to *erubescens* except its foliage is a bit bushier and often ribbed, and there is noticeable light veining down the center that is lacking in *erubescens*. Often crossbred with other philodendrons, *P. tatei* is quite hardy. Work with these philodendrons for success, asset management, new opportunities for expansion, and protection of your assets.

CARE LEVEL: beginner to intermediate

P. hastatum has long, thinner leaves that resemble swords when young; when mature those leaves look more like large spearhead. While the original *hastatum* is a fantastic ally for protection and mental acuity, a cultivar called *P. hastatum* 'Silver Sword' has glossy pale green leaves that look silver, and it is an incredibly helpful ally in all matters of protection, especially of property.

CARE LEVEL: beginner to intermediate

Sansevieria

SNAKE PLANT

Also known as mother-in-law's tongue, devil's tongue, or jinn's tongue, *Sansevieria* was recently reclassified as a species of *Dracaena* on the basis of genetic studies. It is known for its thick, sharp, and hardy leaves that grow upward in a rosette pattern around a growth point. It gets its names from the toughness of the leaves that, in some instances, can actually cut you. It is loved for its succulent, hardy nature and love of neglect, and prefers to be allowed to spread outward through running shoots and enjoy drier conditions, requiring little humidity.

Once its foliage has been damaged, that damage will remain permanently as the leaves will callous over or scar but won't replace lost tissue. If this happens while it is growing, it will often stop putting energy into the damaged leaf and instead put energy into a new one.

REGION OF ORIGIN: Africa, Madagascar, Southern Asia

GROWTH RATE: moderate

HABIT: clumping

DIFFICULTY LEVEL: beginner

GENERAL CARE: Allow their pot to dry out completely before thoroughly watering them. Most are tolerant of low light conditions but prefer bright indirect light. Propagate through division or leaf cutting.

TOXIC: yes

VIBRATIONAL KEYWORDS: protection, defense, removing obstacles

TEMPERAMENT: projective

ELEMENT: air

PLANET: Mercury

ZODIAC: Gemini, Aquarius, Libra

MINERAL: moldavite, kyanite, leopard jasper, chevron amethyst, selenite

TAROT: Queen of Swords

AFFIRMATION: I cut through all obstacles.

MAGICAL EMPLOYMENT: I find *Sansevieria* to be incredibly protective, so much so that I originally assumed them to be fiery and Mars-oriented. However, over time I have grown to see them as mercurial creatures with a knack for strategy and defense. Grow them for general protection but especially protection from spirits that mean you harm, rumors and gossip, and general bad luck. They should be grown near the front or back doors if possible. Additionally, their mercurial traits and ability to tolerate low light also make them a good plant to grow in areas of the home where energy feels trapped or stagnant as their leaves will help to move energy trapped in these locations.

Scindapsus
SATIN POTHOS

Scindapsus often gets confused with *Epipremnum* as they have nearly identical leaf shape and growth habits. There are distinct differences, however. Scindapsus leaves often have a suede texture, their leaves are not a perfectly symmetrical heart shape but rather the tips tend to taper to one side, and there is a great depth of silver in the patterning. Most scindapsus sparkle when under direct light if they have silver variegation, an effect not seen with their cousins. They are mostly root-climbing vines that live deep in the forest.

REGION OF ORIGIN: Southeast Asia and Pacific Islands

GROWTH RATE: moderate

HABIT: vining

DIFFICULTY LEVEL: intermediate

GENERAL CARE: They prefer bright indirect light and rich, well-draining, chunky soil. Like all vining plants, they require a trellis or pole to climb in order to increase leaf size; otherwise, keep them in a hanging basket if you want their leaves to remain small.

TOXIC: yes

VIBRATIONAL KEYWORDS: freedom, untamable nature, the divine feminine

TEMPERAMENT: projective

ELEMENT: water

PLANET: Moon

ZODIAC: Cancer

MINERAL: blue calcite, jade, kyanite, silver, obsidian, onyx, moonstone, labradorite

TAROT: Judgement

AFFIRMATION: I am a magical being.

MAGICAL EMPLOYMENT: I associate these with all lunar deities as their unique coloring makes them look like they are constantly touched with moonlight. I grow them all throughout my office as a way of honoring my personal connection with the moon and the goddess of witches. Work with them to build intuition, to find freedom from oppressive situations, and to discover meaningful personal truths.

Species and Hybrids of Note

There are two species that we are likely to see when looking for scindapsus on the market.

S. pictus and its cultivars have a high amount of silver variegation and their leaves tend to grow larger quicker than similar scindapsus such as the *S. pictus* 'Argyraeus', whose leaves have silver specks. Work with them when you need to break free from oppressive situations and honor the wild within.

CARE LEVEL: beginner

S. treubii has thick, glossy leaves. Its cultivar the *S. treubii* 'Moonlight' has painted silver varigation. Work with these when you are developing your psychic abilities, connecting with the unknown forces within yourself, and studying new forms of witchcraft.

CARE LEVEL: beginner

Syngonium

ARROWHEAD VINE

Syngoniums are one of my favorite houseplants to raise because they are beginner friendly and can be prolific growers. They originally hail from the tropical rainforests of South America, Mexico, and the West Indies and have become a staple for many houseplant enthusiasts. *S. angustatum* grows wild in places like Florida after being introduced in the nineteenth century. Like other aroids, most varieties of syngonium undergo quite the change in leaf shape between juvenile and mature forms. When young, the leaves resemble an arrowhead or a goosefoot—hence the common names. However, when allowed to climb and produce mature leaves, each species has its own special display. The oddball is the *S. chiapense*, a variety whose leaves start off with a closed septum and mature to something resembling a heart shape.

REGION OF ORIGIN: Central and South America

GROWTH RATE: fast

HABIT: climbing

DIFFICULTY LEVEL: beginner

GENERAL CARE: Bright indirect light, well-draining soil, and lots of room to do their thing. Some species prefer soggy soil. Propagate through cutting or division.

TOXIC: yes

VIBRATIONAL KEYWORDS: magic, focus, manifestation, goals

TEMPERAMENT: projective

ELEMENT: air, fire

PLANET: Mercury, Mars

ZODIAC: Aries, Gemini, Virgo

MINERAL: clear and rutilated quartz, labradorite, obsidian, jet

TAROT: The Magician

AFFIRMATION: My will manifests with ease.

MAGICAL EMPLOYMENT: Syngoniums are excellent helpers in an all-purpose kind of way in that they assist in bringing focus to the mind, body, and spirit. I enchant each new leaf as it emerges to manifest a blessing or part of a spell and then read the way it unfurls as a form of divination for that working. They grow quickly and propagate easily, so once a working is successful, I will often cut it and use it to produce a whole new plant that is specifically growing to aid me in that original cause. The possibilities are endless with this easy-growing magical ally.

Species and Hybrids of Note

There are several species of syngonium, and each of them can have dozens of cultivars. Being so easy to work with, I recommend literally any you can get your hands on, as my experience has been they are a very forgiving plant and are excellent at training us in how to grow them. There are a handful that I have had exceptional luck with and would recommend procuring if you have the chance, including the following.

S. podophyllum is the parent to many cultivars and one of the most common species to see on the market. All *podophyllum* are great at helping you achieve your goals and bringing manifestation to your spells. The colorful cultivars 'Berry Allusion', 'Bold Allusion', 'Holly', 'Maria/Maria Allusion', 'White Butterfly', and 'Pink Allusion' are the easiest to find at home improvement stores and supermarkets and tend to be particularly resistant to root issues. The cultivars 'Albo', 'Mojito', 'Batik', 'Godzilla', 'Grey Ghost/Green Spot', and 'Three Kings' each have various white forms of green (and sometimes white) variegation that are excellent for scrying.
CARE LEVEL: beginner

S. wendlandii has lobed leaves and thick white variegation around the veins. It is perfect for magic related to money and financial pursuits.
CARE LEVEL: beginner

S. chiapense has thick, smooth leaves that resemble the shape of a heart. They are excellent for working magic to attract new opportunities and for spells and rituals to attract spirit guides and other allies. They are the most protective of the syngonium.
CARE LEVEL: beginner

S. angustatum is a dark green variety with white variegation around the veins. It grows invasively in many parts of the southern US and Mexico. It is a great ally in dream magic, especially when you want to send someone else images or thoughts in their dreams.
CARE LEVEL: beginner

S. erythrophyllum is a smooth-leafed variety with a dark green top to its foliage and a burgundy bottom. They are particularly good with love magic, especially to attract and draw new lovers or suitors.

CARE LEVEL: beginner

Tradescantia

SPIDERWORT

Tradescantia is one of my favorite plants to grow. Its common names include inch plant, dayflower, and the wandering dude. A high resistance to most pests and a fast-growing nature make this one of the best plants for beginners and anyone who enjoys a splash of color. There are some eighty-five species in this genus, and many are commonly grown throughout the world as an ornamental houseplant. Its leaves are long, thin, and lance-shaped; depending on the species, they can range in color and variegation between silver and purple to green and red.

Like dieffenbachia, it has a rather unfortunate common name; however, this one is rooted in antisemitism. The term "wandering dude" is a newer invention to replace the widely used common name of wandering Jew.

REGION OF ORIGIN: throughout the Americas

GROWTH RATE: fast

HABIT: trailing, crawling

DIFFICULTY LEVEL: beginner

GENERAL CARE: They prefer well-draining soil, bright indirect light (though they do well with a few hours of direct light), and appreciate fertilizer. Propagate by cutting.

TOXIC: mildly toxic to pets

VIBRATIONAL KEYWORDS: healing, recovery

TEMPERAMENT: receptive

ELEMENT: air

PLANET: Mercury

ZODIAC: Libra, Aquarius

MINERAL: Herkimer diamond, bloodstone, amethyst, red jasper, black tourmaline

TAROT: Temperance

AFFIRMATION: I am capable of healing my mind, body, and spirit.

MAGICAL EMPLOYMENT: Tradescantia is a tough plant that lends its energies to health and healing quite easily. In some parts of the world, various species are worked with medicinally to cure a range of ailments. In magic, turn to tradescantia for help with work related to recuperating after illness or surgery and to aid in recovery from addiction.

Species and Hybrids of Note

While they make all-purpose healers, there are certain species that seem to be better at certain aspects of healing than others.

T. blossfeldiana, also known as *T.* 'Nanouk', is a large-leaf species with green and white striped leaves and pinkish-purple blushing. This variety is excellent for aiding in healing bones.
CARE LEVEL: beginner

T. pallida is a large-leaf variety that is purple and is sometimes called the purple heart. It is great for recovery after surgery or severe accidents.

CARE LEVEL: beginner

T. zebrina is the most popular species with its glossy purple, green, and silver leaves. It is especially good in magic for those who are in recovery, are dealing with blood-related illnesses, or are on dialysis.

CARE LEVEL: beginner

Zamioculcas Zamiifolia

ZZ PLANT

The ZZ plant is an oddball whose stems and glossy leaves resemble open bird wings. Its common names include the emerald palm and eternity plant, and it has only been part of the plant scene since the late 1990s, which makes it one of the newer plants on the market. Due to the rhizomes' habit of storing water, it is important that the soil it is planted in be allowed to dry out completely between waterings to avoid root rot. It is a plant known for its durability and hardiness. Allowing for it to dry out like this will also stimulate the plant to produce larger rhizomes with larger stems and leaves. There are only a handful of cultivars at the moment, most notably the black *Zamioculcas zamiifolia* 'Raven' and the 'Super Nova', which is smaller and more compact, with darker than average leaves.

REGION OF ORIGIN: Eastern and Southern Africa

GROWTH RATE: slow to moderate

HABIT: rhizomatous

DIFFICULTY LEVEL: beginner

GENERAL CARE: These plants enjoy well-draining, succulent-type soil and must dry between waterings. Otherwise, they have few needs.

TOXIC: yes

VIBRATIONAL KEYWORDS: communication, breakthroughs

TEMPERAMENT: projective

ELEMENT: air

PLANET: Mercury

ZODIAC: Gemini

MINERAL: clear quartz, agates, topaz, sodalite, tiger's eye

TAROT: Knight of Swords

AFFIRMATION: I speak clearly with the spirit world.

MAGICAL EMPLOYMENT: ZZ plants are amazing at aiding in spirit guide communication and when working to understand messages from the spirit world. Grow them near the altar or where you do readings to bring clarity and depth to messages from the other side.

Conclusion

At the start of this book, I mentioned that my partner and I are the caretakers of over twelve hundred indoor plants. We are lucky enough to have space to do so and people we live with who like the look and feel of having plants in our shared spaces, especially as long as they don't have to be responsible for them. That number may sound astronomical to you, and I suppose it is, but we amassed this jungle for a reason: plants make life better. We participate in rescue and conservation efforts for species that are going extinct in the wild, we trade cuttings with other growers, we import plants from small family operations and coops overseas, and we are quite chummy with our local plant shops. It all just sort of happened organically over several years, and we found ourselves part of a wonderful network of people who are just like us—plant people who want to make life better one stem at a time. We didn't set out to have a large collection; we just eventually ended up with one.

You may not find yourself with twelve hundred plants—actually, you probably don't want to find yourself with that many plants as they are a lot of work—but as a collector and magical indoor gardening enthusiast, you should always feel empowered to work with the collection you do have. Plants are not a commodity; they aren't a resource for us to exploit. Whether we are fully conscious of that or not, they are our companions; we rely on them, and those that we bring into our homes rely on us. Inviting them into your magical practice as participants, teachers, and allies is, however, the bonus that comes with caring for them. The real payoff and magic is in watching them grow and growing with them.

In these pages we have explored the all-pervading force that fuels plant life, the green flame, as a potent source of magic. We discussed how to find it and how to bring it into every facet of our lives. We learned how to identify the magical properties within our houseplants as well as how to care for them so that they not only survive but thrive. We have also learned how to anchor the everyday and long-term spiritual benefits of this work into our lives in meaningful ways. If you responded to the journal prompts in the green gnosis sections at the end of each chapter in part 1, you also have the beginnings of your own book of magical lessons and secrets from the plant kingdom. Read over your notes and responses, find inspiration in your own words, and approach the next plant you bring home with confidence.

I don't believe in goodbyes and farewells, so instead I want to invite you to join me online at ModernWitch.com. There I work with a team of folks to create a safe, positive, and nurturing magical space for witches and occultists of all kinds. We even have a special home for green witches and an annual teaching event called HortOCCULTure, from which this book gets its name. If you are hungry for more green magic or just magic in general, come join us.

Until then, I leave you with this blessing:

May your stems grow firm,
your foliage be bright, and
your roots remain strong.

APPENDIX | Plants by Habitat

Pet-Friendly Houseplants

African violet (*Saintpaulia*)
Baby tears (*Soleirolia soleirolii*)
Banana (*Musa* spp.)
Bird's nest fern *(Asplenium nidus)*
Boston fern (*Nephrolepsis exaltata*)
Butterfly palm *(Dypsis lutescens)*
Button fern (*Pellaea rotundifolia*)
Calathea (*Calathea* spp.)
Echeveria (*Echeveria* spp.)
Maidenhair fern (*Adiantum* spp.)
Parlor palm (*Chamaedorea elegans*)
Peacock plant *(Calathea* spp.)
Peperomia *(Peperomia* spp.)
Pilea (*Pilea peperomioides*)
Ponytail palm (*Beaucarnea recurvata*)
Prayer plant (*Maranta* spp.)
Spider plant (*Chlorophytum comosum*)
Staghorn fern (*Platycerium bifurcatum*)

Venus flytrap (*Dionaea muscipula*)
Wax plants (*Hoya* spp.)

Low-Light Tolerant Houseplants

Arrowhead vine (*Syngonium* spp.)
Cast-iron plant (*Aspidistra* spp.)
Dieffenbachia (*Dieffenbachia* spp.)
Dragon tree (*Dracaena marginata*)
English ivy (*Hedera helix*)
False aralia (*Plerandra elegantissima*)
Fiddle-leaf fig (*Ficus lyrata*)
Lucky bamboo (*Dracaena sanderiana*)
Monstera (*Monstera deliciosa*)
Parlor palm (*Chamaedorea elegans*)
Peace lily (*Spathiphyllum* spp.)
Pothos (*Epipremnum aureum*)
Schefflera (*Schefflera* spp.)
Silver pothos (*Scindapsus pictus*)
Snake plant (*Sansevieria trifasciata*)
Spider plant (*Chlorophytum comosum*)
Staghorn fern (*Platycerium bifurcatum*)
Swiss cheese plant (*Monstera adansonii*)
Tradescantia (*Tradescantia zebrina*)
Weeping fig (*Ficus benjamina*)
ZZ plant (*Zamioculcas zamiifolia*)

Plants That Stay Small

African violets (*Saintpaulia*)
Air plants (*Tillandsia* spp.)
Alocasia (*Alocasia amazonica* 'Polly')
Aloe (*Aloe vera*)

Baby tears (*Soleirolia soleirolii*)
Button fern (*Pellaea rotundifolia*)
Cape primrose (*Streptocarpus* spp.)
Chinese evergreen (*Aglaonema* spp.)
Echeveria (*Echeveria* spp.)
Lithops (*Lithops* spp.)
Lucky bamboo (*Dracaena sanderiana*)
Nerve plant (*Fittonia* spp.)
Peperomia (*Peperomia* spp.)
Pilea (*Pilea peperomioides*)
Polka-dot plant (*Hypoestes phyllostachya*)
Shamrock (*Oxalis* spp.)
String of pearls (*Senacia* spp.)
Venus flytrap (*Dionaea muscipula*)
Wax plant (*Hoya* spp.)
Zebra haworthia (*Haworthiopsis fasciata*)

NASA-Approved Plants That Improve Air Quality

Bamboo palm (*Chamaedorea seifritzii*)
Chinese evergreen (*Aglaonema modestum*)
Corn plant (*Dracaena fragans*)
Dragon tree (*Dracaena marginata*)
English ivy (*Hedera helix*)
Gerbera daisy (*Gerbera jamesonii*)
Peace lily (*Spathiphyllum* spp.)
Pothos (*Scindapsus aureum*)
Pot mum (*Chrysanthemum × morifolium*)
Snake plant (*Sansevieria trifasciata*)
Spider plant (*Chlorophytum comosum*)
Weeping fig (*Ficus benjamina*)

Glossary

AERIAL ROOT—Roots emerging from an aboveground node that stabilize the growing plant.

AROIDS—Members of the Araceae family including alocasia, anthurium, philodendrons, monsteras, scindapsus, and zamioculcas. Aroids are known for their growth habit as well as their inflorescence consisting of a spathe and a spadix.

CATAPHYLL—Modified leaf structure that does not produce photosynthesis but rather is formed as a protective structure for emerging leaves.

CAUDEX—A specialized trunk or aboveground root system that evolved to allow plants to store water in harsh conditions.

CHLOROSIS—Discoloring (yellowing or fading) of the leaves associated with a lack of chlorophyl production. Usually a sign of root struggle (overwatering, underwatering, or becoming compact in pot) or pest infestation.

CULTIVAR—A plant that was bred specifically by humans.

DICOT—One of two major classifications of flowering plants, distinguished by growth habit where (among several other distinguishing features) these plants emerge from a seed containing two embryonic leaves. These plants have flowering petals that come in sets of four or five and leaves with scatter or reticulated veins. Examples are begonia and ficus.

EPIPHYTE—A plant that has evolved to grow on other plants (like trees), without soil, usually in a non-parasitic way.

FAMILY—A taxonomical grouping of plants based on shared characteristics and genetic heritage.

FENESTRATION—Holes and splits in leaves that resemble windows, believed to have evolved to allow for wind to move through larger leaves without damaging them.

GENUS—A subcategory of family, denoting shared characteristics among species.

HABIT—General appearance and structure.

HYBRID—Offspring produced by crossing two different species within the same genus.

HYDROPONIC—Soilless cultivation of plants wherein nutrients are delivered through water-based minerals and aqueous solvents.

INFLORESCENCE—The complete flowering head of a plant, including stem, spathe, spadix, and flowers.

INTERNODE—The stem portion between nodes.

LITHOPHYTE—Plants that have evolved to grow on rocks or in rocky substrate.

LOBE—Referring to the projections that emerge from the midrib of a leaf.

MONOCOT—One of two major classifications of flowering plants, distinguished by growth habit where (among several other distinguishing features) these plants emerge from a seed containing one embryonic leaf. These plants have flowering petals that come in sets of three and leaves with parallel running veins. Examples are all aroids, gingers, and bamboos.

NODE—A lumpy part of the stem containing the entire genetic material of the plant. Nodes are identified as areas where petioles and (aerial) roots emerge.

PEDUNCLE—The main stalk of an inflorescence bearing a single flower or a cluster of flowers (as seen in hoyas).

PETIOLE—A minor stem that connects the blade of a leaf to the stem or stalk of a plant.

PH—Referring to the acidity/alkalinity of soil.

RETICULATED—Veining leaf pattern that resembles a network or interlacing lines.

RHIZOME—A grouping of underground stems that create both roots and shoots.

SEMI-HYDROPONIC—A method for cultivation blending traditional and hydroponic wherein plants are rooted in clay or mineral aggregates and fed nutrients through aqueous solutions. LECA (lightweight expanded clay aggregate) and pon (small mixed mineral aggregates) are popular forms of semi-hydroponic substrate.

SEPTUM—The part of a leaf blade where two lobes meet and the petiole connects.

SPADIX—A fleshy stem containing several small flowers.

SPATHE—A modified leaf, often colorful, that acts as a protective sheath for the spadix. Often the spadix and spathe are confused as a single flower.

SPECIES—A further classification of plants within a genus based on characteristics.

SUBSTRATE—The medium in which we grow plants.

SUCCULENT—Plants that have evolved in extreme conditions and have developed the ability to store water for long periods of time.

Bibliography and Recommended Reading

Auryn, Mat. *Psychic Witch: A Metaphysical Guide to Meditation, Magick & Manifestation*. Llewellyn, 2020.

———. *Mastering Magick: A Course in Spellcasting for the Psychic Witch*. Llewellyn, 2022.

Blackthorn, Amy. *Blackthorn's Botanical Magic: The Green Witch's Guide to Essential Oils for Spellcraft, Ritual, and Healing*. Weiser, 2018.

———. *Blackthorn's Botanical Brews: Herbal Potions, Magical Teas, and Spirited Libations*. Weiser, 2020.

———. *Blackthorn's Botanical Wellness: A Green Witch's Guide to Self-Care*. Weiser, 2022.

Bogan, Chas. *The Secret Keys of Conjure: Unlocking the Mysteries of American Folk Magic*. Llewellyn, 2018.

Camilleri, Lauren, and Sophia Kaplan. *Plantopedia: The Definitive Guide to Houseplants*. Smith Street Books, 2020.

Cunningham, Scott. *Cunningham's Encyclopedia of Magical Herbs*. Llewellyn, 1985.

———. *Earth, Air, Fire & Water: More Techniques of Natural Magic*. Llewellyn, 1991.

Diaz, Juliet. *Witchery: Embrace the Witch Within*. Hay House, 2019.

———. *Plant Witchery: Discover the Sacred Language, Wisdom, and Magic of 200 Plants*. Hay House, 2021.

———. *The Altar Within: A Radical Devotional Guide to Liberate the Divine Self*. Row House, 2022.

Dominguez, Ivo, Jr. *Spirit Speak: Knowing and Understanding Spirit Guides, Ancestors, Ghosts, Angels, and the Divine*. New Page Books, 2008.

———. *The Four Elements of the Wise: Working with the Magickal Powers of Earth, Air, Water, Fire*. Weiser, 2021.

Faerywolf, Storm. *The Witch's Name: Crafting Identities of Magical Power*. Llewellyn, 2022.

Horst, Danae. *Houseplants for All: How to Fill Any Home with Happy Plants*. Illustrated edition. Harvest, 2020.

Hunter, Devin. *The Witch's Book of Power*. Llewellyn, 2016.

———. *The Witch's Book of Spirits*. Llewellyn, 2017.

———. *The Witch's Book of Mysteries*. Llewellyn, 2019.

———. *Modern Witch: Spells, Recipes & Workings*. Llewellyn, 2020.

———. *Crystal Magic for the Modern Witch*. Llewellyn, 2022.

Illes, Judika. *Encyclopedia of 5000 Spells*. Illustrated edition. Harper One, 2009.

———. *Encyclopedia of Witch Craft: The Complete A–Z for the Entire Magical World*. Harper One, 2014.

Kramer, Jack. *Pocket Guide to Houseplants: Over 240 Easy-Care Favorites*. Creative Homeowner, 2019.

Kynes, Sandra. *Plant Magic: A Year of Green Wisdom for Pagans & Wiccans*. Llewellyn, 2017.

Michael, Coby. *The Poison Path Herbal: Baneful Herbs, Medicinal Nightshades, and Ritual Entheogens.* Park Street Press, 2021.

Moura, Ann (Aoumiel). *Green Magic: The Sacred Connection to Nature.* Llewellyn, 2002.

———. *Green Witchcraft: Folk Magic, Fairy Lore & Herb Craft.* Green Witchcraft series, 1. Llewellyn, 2002.

———. *Grimoire for the Green Witch: A Complete Book of Shadows* (Green Witchcraft series, 5). Llewellyn, 2003.

Murphy-Hiscock, Arin. *The Green Witch's Grimoire: Your Complete Guide to Creating Your Own Book of Natural Magic.* Adams Media, 2020.

———. *The Green Witch's Garden: Your Complete Guide to Creating and Cultivating a Magical Garden Space.* Adams Media, 2021.

Peerless, Veronica. *How Not to Kill Your Houseplant: Survival Tips for the Horticulturally Challenged.* DK, 2017.

Penczak, Christopher. *The Outer Temple of Witchcraft: Circles, Spells, and Rituals.* Penczak Temple series, 4. Llewellyn, 2004.

———. *The Plant Spirit Familiar.* Copper Cauldron Publishing, 2011.

Pollack, Rachel. *Seventy-Eight Degrees of Wisdom.* Second edition. Thorsons, 1998.

RavenWolf, Silver. *Solitary Witch: The Ultimate Book of Shadows for the New Generation.* Llewellyn, 2003.

———. *HedgeWitch: Spells, Crafts & Rituals for Natural Magick.* Llewellyn, 2008.

Sédir, Paul, and R. Bailey. *Occult Botany: Sédir's Concise Guide to Magical Plants.* Inner Traditions, 2021.

Index

To Write to the Author

If you wish to contact the author or would like more information about this book, please write to the author in care of Llewellyn Worldwide and we will forward your request. Both the author and the publisher appreciate hearing from you and learning of your enjoyment of this book and how it has helped you. Llewellyn Worldwide cannot guarantee that every letter written to the author can be answered, but all will be forwarded. Please write to:

Devin Hunter
℅ Llewellyn Worldwide
2143 Wooddale Drive
Woodbury, MN 55125-2989

Please enclose a self-addressed stamped envelope for reply or $1.00 to cover costs. If outside the USA, enclose an international postal reply coupon.

Many of Llewellyn's authors have websites with additional information and resources. For more information, please visit our website:

WWW.LLEWELLYN.COM